escape

velocity

REVOLUTIONARY BUSINESS STRATEGY FOR
SURVIVAL IN A WORLD OF UNPRECENDENTED
COMPETITIVE INTENSITY AND
ACCELERATED CHANGE.

Idris Mootee

Knowledge Capital Publishing

About this book

This book is written for management consultants as well as senior executives working in one of the most challenging of times - a time of unprecedented competitive intensity and relentlessly accelerating change. The turmoil we are experiencing is undermining all the recipes for success that business schools have taught us. In this book, the author not only explains the pro and cons of different strategy tools and their application in different scenarios, but also looks at the deep theory of strategy creation. Companies and all organizations today face the same compelling question: What is strategy? How should strategy be created? The conventional rules of strategy and management dictate that success is achieved by establishing and maintaining stability, by visualizing a strategic goal, and then basing all strategic planning on its achievement. Here the author proposes alternative concepts as he argues that one cannot succeed using conventional orderly strategies in a highly disorderly world. Using insights from the new sciences of complexity theory, the author brings together a number of practical ideas and shows the promise? These hold for organizing for superior performance. This book crisply argues the need for a radically new approach to strategy. Start-ups and established players alike can harness the author's powerful framework and practical ideas to help their organizations to escape velocity.

escape

velocity

REVOLUTIONARY BUSINESS STRATEGY FOR
SURVIVAL IN A WORLD OF UNPRECENDENTED
COMPETITIVE INTENSITY AND
ACCELERATED CHANGE.

Idris Mootee

"If you keep looking through the prism of diminishing returns, **equilibrium** markets and rational problem-solutions economics, you won't be able to understand this economy at all."

Brian Arthur

"Most organizations are not designed, they **grow**. Indeed, there are several studies which draw on biological analogies to describe organizational phenomena. But not all organizations adapt equally well to the environment within which they grow. Many, like the dinosaur of great size but little brain, remain unchanged in a changing world."

Charles Handy

Copyright 1999 Idris Mootee.

All rights reserved. No part of this work covered by the copyrights heron may be reproduced or used in any form or by any means – graphic, electronic or mechanical, including photocopying, recording, taping or information storage and retrieval systems – without prior written permission from the publisher except in the case of brief quotations embodied in critical articles and reviews. For information please contact Knowledge Capital Publishing Group. Published simultaneously in the United States of America.

A previous privately circulated edition of this book called *From Competitive Advantage to Complexity Theory* was published in 1998.

Canadian Cataloging Publication Data

Mootee, Idris.

    Escape Velocity : Revolutionary Business Strategy for Survival in a World of Unprecedented Competitive Intensity and Accelerated Change

Includes bibliographical references and index

ISBN : 0-9685477-0-2

1. Strategy   2. Strategic Planning   3. Corporate Strategy
4. Management   I. Title

HD188.266.8988–dc233

First Edition

Front cover design by Ken Dutton, San Francisco.
Text design by Alan Evans, Wow Design Group, New York.
Editing by Kate Ng, London.

Printed and bound in Canada.

99 00 9

contents

	Introduction	
	Acknowledgement	
1.	Strategy is only a printed document	1
2.	Assumptions assumptions	14
3.	Exploring the roots of strategy	26
4.	Who needs a strategy?	39
5.	The heart of strategy: the equilibrium systems	48
6.	The new science of complexity theory	61
7.	The growth of complexity	76
8.	Back to strategy	96
9.	The competencies and knowledge landscape	117
10.	Strategy as a guided evolutionary process	147
11.	Practical lessons from the natural world	142
	A thought in closing	159
	Glossary	166
	Reference	171
	Index	175

Acknowledgment

The idea of this book first emerged two years ago while I was chatting with the CEO of a Silicon Valley based company on an evening flight from New York to London. He was telling me how he needed to tell his managers every morning about the strategy of the day. Every day, the company was facing new entrants trying to redefine the rules of competition and create new industries, unconstrained by the dogmas and conventions of the past.

We have generations of MBAs exhorted to sustain competitive advantage or increase commitment by investing in large plants and equipment, who may find today's business reality rather harsh. Today's strengths become tomorrow's weaknesses and today's strategic assets become tomorrow's strategic burden. We have been taught in business schools to select a generic strategy, such as either being a low cost producer or a differentiator. But firms combining advanced e-commerce and manufacturing technologies can maneuver between these positions or occupy both at the same time. Many companies suffer "genetic blindness" as a result of having too many executives in the same industry for too long. Today strategy means looking beyond industry trends and existing structures for clues to tomorrow's opportunities. Successful companies must perceive an almost continuous atmosphere of revolution to create new opportunities, reshape industry and market boundaries, eliminate constraining dogmas and ultimately be able to escape velocity.

This book is an attempt to distill the learning of my past ten years in strategy consulting, working with clients from diverse industries in three continents. I have had the privilege of working with some very knowledgeable client groups who have brought to our relationship not only great problems but wonderful insights into how to solve them. This book would not have been possible without the help of a large number of people including theoretical physicists, chemical scientists, microbiologists and management theorists, all of whom generously shared with me their knowledge and insights, to help me to develop a richer understanding of the new sciences. I would like to express my gratitude to all of them. Also to all those people with whom I crossed paths at London Business School, Harvard Business School and Western Business School and through whom my learning experience has been greatly enriched. I am immensely grateful to my professors at London Business School, whose lively debates and inspiring lectures have shaped much of my thinking. In particular, the opportunity to learn from John Stopford and Sumantra Ghoshal who were well known as the Eurogurus.

And then there are those truly wonderful people at BDC Consulting Group, McKinsey and Co., Strategic Capital Partners, Bratch Innovation, Gemini Consulting, Quantum Knight and Barron, and all those who took the time to read the earlier draft and to critique and advance the argument of this book. They include Steve Lerman, Gill Pratt, Larry Weber, Bruce Cooke, Alan Kay, Bill Sawakaski, Henry Fuchs, Lana Moen, Kwong-Wing Law, Nigel Nicholson, Mark

Weiser, John Brown, Bill Mitchell and Dave Johnson. There are far too many to mention here. Let me simply express my warm appreciation to all of you.

Finally my deepest thanks go to Kate Ng for playing the dual role of developmental editor and copy-editor and putting so many days into this project, and to Michael without whose kind co-operation this would not have been possible.

And finally, I would like to thank my family for putting up with the twelve months of writing – much of it on their time. And the sheer joy they have brought to my life.

Chapter 1

Strategy is only a printed document

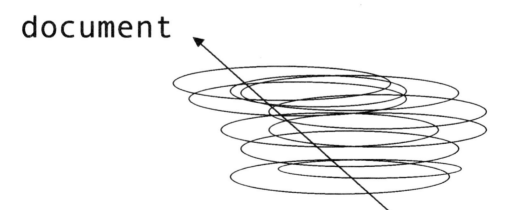

Strategy is only a printed document.

Today's business environment requires a vibrant approach to strategy. The traditional process of devising and implementing strategy on a periodic basis could well be a recipe for disaster given the rapidly changing business conditions and competitive landscape. Everywhere we see companies spending enormous resources only to arrive at a strategy that most of the time becomes a printed document gathering dust on a shelf, or even worse, the major cause of failure. Why? Companies fail because over the last twenty years they have been taught to fail. Imagine Joe Stalin visits Corporate America: "Now we have a five-year plan. The five-year plan is all in a three-ring binder. The three-ring binder is on a shelf in the CEO's as well as all senior executives' offices. The five-year plan sets out our visions, goals and directions. Assuming the future is predictable, we will meet or exceed those goals." In this all-too-familiar model, the pieces of the company and the pieces of the strategy are broken down into separate elements. Line is separate from staff. Market research has nothing to do with product positioning. There is little or no connection between strategy and operations. Companies then decompose pieces of their strategy into separate mini-projects and assign them out to different people in different places - people who have never worked together, never even met each other. In fact, these people were hired, promoted, motivated, and rewarded in ways that trained them not to like each other, not to trust each other, not to help each other, not to speak to each other. Very often they were all trained or encouraged by the systems not to work together. The company is fragmented by what I call "Internal White Space."

An example of internal white space

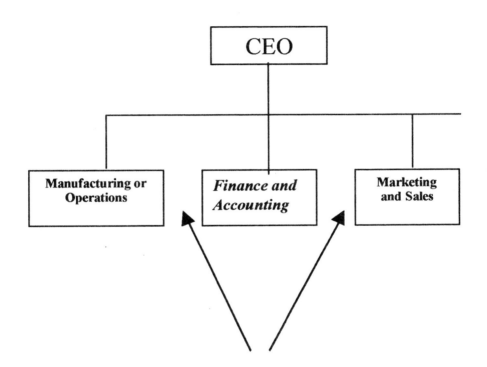

In this respect, right through the Vietnam War, big companies and the military shared much the same approach to strategy. Both labored under institutional dynamics that virtually guaranteed competitive defeat. The terrible irony of Vietnam was that the United States won almost every single battle but lost the war. The same thing happened during the Desert Storm: Although the United States did win the war this time, it still has not achieved what it intended. The same happened to the war over Kosovo. We see the same phenomenon in American business. Many companies won every market share battle but missed the industry breakpoints where value shifted to new entrants. Most military histories of the Vietnam War agree on the reason for defeat - the military had no unified strategic doctrine, no clear definition of victory. American business had its Vietnam ten years after the Pentagon did. In the 1980s, one company after another confronted agile domestic competitors and new global rivals. These "guerrillas" exposed the flaws of business-as-usual. Like the Pentagon, business learned its lesson the hard way. Maybe it is time for us to learn to change.

If we take a good look at today's organizations in any industry it is not unusual to find managers caught up in the rivalry between competitive firms, competitive partners and competitive suppliers on a day-to-day basis. It would be a natural instinct to see rivalry as the centerpiece of strategy. Yet if we take a historical perspective, the most dynamic changes in industry structure and business performance have always been driven by innovation; what Schumpeter calls the

"Gale of Creative Destruction." We are now on the verge of a phase transition between the old economic order and the new. Businesses and industries all over the world are entering a period of unprecedented and seemingly permanent volatility and turbulence. Everyone is inevitably facing global megatrends such as the explosive and accelerating power of information and communications technologies. These newly converging technologies are shattering organizational barriers, empowering new players and completely reinventing or rewriting the rules of every industry's game. The rapid globalization of markets, competition, trading patterns and finance capital have resulted in the emergence of knowledge-based industries. The explosion and convergence of computing, communications and financial technologies have created a world of instantaneous interdependence. There is a fundamental shift from a world economy very much based on manufacturing and natural resource exploitation to one based on knowledge and information. The company who can pull away from its competition is this environment is the one that can rapidly and continuously reinvent itself.

Unfortunately many organizations and even business schools have not yet made the transition to the new economic model. Strategic plans that sometimes take two or three years to develop are useless before they are even finished.

Business competition is fluid and fast changing and companies need to gather intelligence constantly - covering a wide range of considerations. They need to go beyond conventional approaches to strategy that map only financial and physical assets. In an economy where human assets, skills, knowledge of customers or certain processes, software, and technologies are the critical weapons, companies must map them as well.

> "We've got to live with chaos and uncertainty, to try to be comfortable with it and not to look for certainty where we **won't** get it."
>
> Charles Handy

A typical large company has what it considers perfectly suitable maps. It has an organization chart, which the company would consider a map of its executives. It has a mission statement, an income statement and a balance sheet, which the company would consider a map of its financial resources. It may even have a map of its physical assets: factories, offices, labs etc. Let us think about the maps companies don't have - the maps that would support informed choices. For example, most companies don't have a single useful map of their human resources. One company that I consulted with a few years back made a bold strategic decision to preempt the competition by dominating the market for its product in China. Yes, a timely decision. But did the company have any data - a map - that would determine how many of its managers had lived or worked in China? How many spoke Chinese? How many would be willing to commit to relocate to China with their families for five years? Unfortunately in their case, not too many. Which meant that after the CEO had made his bold, timely decision, the company discovered it was short of some 300 people to implement it. Another company - a large financial institution - decided to target the high growth knowledge-based business sector. The management launched a huge effort only to discover that their team did not know a thing about the financial challenges facing these companies. Uninformed choice, and no action. Companies without relevant maps - or companies that don't update their maps to keep them dynamic and accurate - are destined to repeat this sort of strategic blunder.

Now consider maps of a company's intellectual assets. Almost everyone agrees that we work in a knowledge-based economy, and among academics and consultants there is much talk of "knowledge management." But most companies have never considered mapping their knowledge assets, or have yet to find a way of mapping them. How many companies map their patent activity in a product category against the competition? Over years, patent maps can produce remarkable insights into the trajectory of new product development by rivals. Virtually every "killer product" or "killer application" emerges from a point on the map where a company has concentrated its patents. A patent map can serve as an early warning system for competitors' new-product intentions. And finally, how many companies even make the effort to find out about their core competencies, not to mention trying to map them? And yet core competencies are often regarded as being at the heart of value creation.

How many organizations map their Human Assets, Core -Competencies or Customer Insights?

How much does an organization chart tell you about a company?

NOT MUCH

The point is that informed choice starts with accurate, dynamic and real-time information. When top executives get information that cuts across boundaries, they begin to see previously hidden interconnections between functions and divisions. Integrated information enables integrated decisions. It allows lateral and intuitive thinking which is ripe for innovation.

To make any kind of change, companies need a new framework that guides people at all levels as they convert informed choice into timely action. In military terms, they need corporate doctrine.

The idea of "Doctrine of Management" first came to my mind when a professor of mine at London Business School, Sumantra Ghoshal, first raised the idea in a class. Each one of us was asked to write his or her own "Management Doctrine." Surprisingly the idea had never occurred to anyone in the class, which consisted mostly of senior international executives with an average of ten to fifteen years management experience. And so it was from many other previous classes I was told. Doctors, lawyers - almost all professions are bound together by a common language and code of practice. But no such doctrine forms part of a manager's training. And we had never really thought about the way we practice our profession. Doctrine is fundamental to war. As defined in "Warfighting," the Marine Corps' handbook on strategy and operations, doctrine is "the fundamental beliefs of the Marine Corps on the subject of war, from its nature and theory to its preparation and conduct. Doctrine establishes a particular way of thinking about war and a way of fighting, a philosophy for leading Marines into combat, a mandate for professionalism, and a common language. In short, it establishes the way we practice our profession."

What would be your own "**Doctrine**" of Management if you were to write one?

In business and management, doctrine is still waiting to be created. Almost all executives accept the need for formal strategies to define the means by which companies compete. Most executives have embraced mission, vision, and values to communicate the ends for which companies compete. Still, something is missing here: the doctrine that provides the integration between ends and means - how companies compete. Should we call it "Strategy"?

Doctrine is not minutely prescriptive. In the case of the military, it does not provide detailed instructions on how to fight specific campaigns. Rather, it is a mixture of philosophy ("maneuver warfare," says Warfighting, "is a way of thinking in and about war that should shape our every action") and practice (subordinates "should understand the intent of the commander two levels up") and the connections between the two. During the first year after the Gulf war, the US Army was subjected to severe stress as a result of downsizing and redeployment from Europe. They discovered that the best way to sustain an acceptable level of readiness was to make the initial stages of transformation as transparent as possible. They believed that without a solid intellectual foundation upon which to build all training, education, leadership development and organization design, the Army could easily become disoriented and unprepared. And within just two years, their work on doctrine had already yielded a new capstone field manual, FM100-5. This defined the Army operations at the highest level. The doctrine included important work on strategic deployment and peacekeeping operations that had never before been published.

In business and management, good doctrine meets three needs. First, it establishes a common purpose - the company's definition of victory. Second, it establishes a common language - a shared way of expressing the corporate strategy. Third, it establishes common decision rules - a shared framework for action. The sum of these elements answers the questions that any company must answer if it expects to win: How do we compete? Where do we compete? How do we conduct ourselves? How do we know whether we're winning or losing?

In the present business world competition has become so ferocious, multifaceted and unpredictable that no competitive advantage can possibility be sustainable. Competitive advantage must be constantly be re-created. We are in a time where continuous innovation - a constant commitment to change - is an essential ingredient to organizational success and, even more fundamentally, to survival. This is very much in contrast to popular management theories based on Newtonian and cognitive assumptions, which have had limited success in helping us to understand firms in the knowledge economy, where continuous adaptation is a necessary condition for long-term and maybe even medium-term survival.

To escape velocity it is vital that managers develop competencies that allow them not just to see, but also to understand and be able to shape situations in new ways and navigate in chaotic systems - to see change as an opportunity. This book is written to help managers understand how they can think about strategy and how they can begin to think about it differently. It is an attempt to establish why so much taken-for-granted-knowledge that may not actually be firmly embedded in the rock of truth and why this shifting foundation means there may be other ways to approach strategy that might be more useful or appropriate at times. In this book, I will invite you to explore different dimensions of strategy in a way that can transform your thinking about strategy and your organization. It will challenge you to see and think anew. It will explain to you the roots of many management and strategy concepts. It will expose you to the latest in management thinking from across many different disciplines and show how we can transcend the constraints of traditional assumptions about competition and strategy to develop a more disciplined approach. It will attempt to translate the new sciences of complexity theory and evolutionary theory into practical management, and demonstrate the usefulness of these approaches which offer vastly different implications about ways of competing and even the definition of strategy itself.

Asking a management theorist to define **strategy** is rather like asking a philosopher to define truth.

In short, this book will breathe **new** life into your strategy making process.

Chapter 2

Assumptions
Assumptions

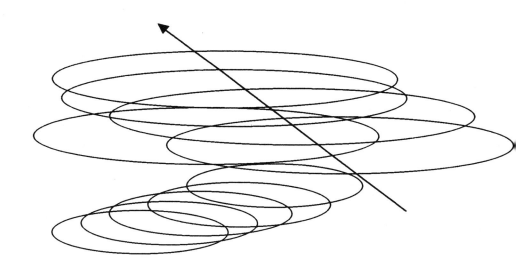

At the heart of all strategies are some basic assumptions. Strategic planners assume that management can make growth as one builds a house or a machine. The resulting models lead to the formulation of strategic plans which totally ignore human behavior and the changing environment.

THEORY is where you know everything but nothing actually works; **PRACTICE** is where everything works but no one knows how.

Why is that some firms seem to be able to adapt sufficiently well to their industry changes and survive, while others simply fail or become extinct? What has happened to the list of fine and widely admired companies observed by Tom Peters in his book "In Search of Excellence(1982)"? Management theory to date has been unable to explain why some organizations are stubbornly unwilling to adapt while others have survived for hundreds of years. It seems to me that companies that perceive themselves as excellent are particularly prone to fail. For years strategic planners at corporate giants such as IBM and GM failed to see their own impending demise. Focused exclusively on their own measures of corporate performance – the manipulatable objects of their metaphorical models – they were blind to changing behaviors among users, within the organization and all along the value chain.

The story is quite a familiar one: a company that only yesterday was a superstar or a company of excellence finds itself stagnating and frustrated, in trouble, and frequently in a seemingly unmanageable crisis. This phenomenon is by no means confined to organizations in the United States. It has become common in Japan, Korea, Germany, France and Sweden. And it occurs just as often outside business - in labor unions, government agencies, hospitals, museums, and churches. In fact, it seems even less tractable in those areas.

There has been a proliferation of tools and techniques to help organizations manage their way out of crises: downsizing, outsourcing, total quality management, economic value analysis, balanced scorecard, benchmarking, business process reengineering etc. But so far there has been scant evidence of any enduring successes attributable to these approaches.

To develop lasting solutions, we need a far more profound understanding of root causes. The root cause of nearly every one of these crises is not that things are being done badly. It is not even that the wrong things are being done. Indeed, in most cases, the right things are being done – but fruitlessly. What accounts for this apparent paradox? The assumptions on which the organization has been built and is being run no longer fit reality. These are the assumptions that shape any organization's behavior, dictate its decisions about what to do and what not to do, and define what the organization considers meaningful results. These assumptions are about markets and customers. They are about identifying strategic alliances and competitors, and their values and behavior. They are about technological changes and its dynamics, about a company's strengths and weaknesses. They are about what a company gets paid for. They are what Peter Drucker call a company's theory of the business. Every organization, whether a business or not, has a theory of the business. But theory is a construct; it is not truth. When reality shifts, the theories we used to explain it, begin to lose their validity.

> "Some theories of the business are so powerful that they last for a long time. But being human artifacts they don't last forever, and, indeed, today they **rarely** last for long at all."
>
> Peter Drucker, The Theory of Business

It is here that I try to journey through in this book, proposing that the reason for the frequent failure of many remedies for change lies in their use of assumptions with limited validity in the organizational and business context of today's knowledge economy. I believe that many management theories and "remedies" can focus only on the relatively superficial level of managerial practices and "artifacts" which in turn reduces their explanatory power. In fact, I would place most of the best selling how to books on Business Process Re-engineering and Change Management in this category, and a number of surveys had shown that CEOs characterize Business Process Reengineering's success as mixed, at best.

Business Process Reengineering has been one of the hottest ideas in North American business for a good ten years. Its aims are clear: increased competitiveness and profitability via simpler, leaner, more productive business systems and processes. Its methods are also clear: cross-functional teams, mapping, benchmarking, learning from front-line employees, customer input, throwing out old paradigms in favor of new. Most major firms have reengineered at least some parts of their business - usually with visible and dramatic impact. The typical story goes like this: First managers applied the reengineering concept to the basic routines of the business, bringing about improvements in effectiveness and productivity. Greater speed and reduced headcount followed. Building on success, firms then extended the reengineering concept, and what started as reengineering of just order processing became a reassessment of all customer service.

But at this point, besides asking how to do it better, one must also determine what to do and for whom to do it. These are classic strategy choices, and it's vital to get them right. Unfortunately, much of the reengineering methodology has trouble coping with these important questions.

> It is relatively easy to rearrange the deck chairs on the sinking Titanic – but **what** is the purpose?

While benchmarking works well for bringing inside the best practices of others, it often amounts to strategy by mimicry. It's not very good for devising an original best practice that doesn't already exist. Cross-functional teams are good at pooling existing knowledge, breaking down barriers, and finding new ways to work inside the existing game. But these same teams often shy away from more speculative data gathering, "blue sky" brainstorming and going "outside the box" to change the rules of the game itself. Few team members want to risk embarrassment and failure by going out on a limb that others may not even be able to perceive. Yet this is often exactly what is required to create a strong and original strategy. And so it is that the reengineers are rediscovering the need for strategy.

A question I often ask my clients is: "Now the trains are running and are running on time, where should they go?" That's the question more and more firms are facing even after their reengineering efforts are done. Finding the answer takes more than just reengineering. It takes strategy.

And when we know where our trains are going and that they are running on time, the next question is how to get there. For much of the eighties we looked to the behavioral sciences for our change management models. Lessons from psychology have since confirmed that the ways that people change are more complicated than behaviorists' stimulus-response models supposed. A few approaches such as culture change do attempt to look at organizational values, but virtually none seem to examine managerial assumptions about the meaning of strategy, organization and management

Several researchers studying both change and broader organizational science literature have attempted to uncover some fundamental assumptions that pervade this work, through a process of de-construction. Reflecting the complex adaptive systems paradigm, Stacey (1995) has extensively analyzed many existing management literatures for assumptions that links to Newtonian physics and Darwinian evolution. In a 1995 research paper, he identifies importantly three major assumptions underlying almost every approach to the management of change, or "central evolutionary and transformational processes."

- First, there are clear-cut connections between cause and effect, therefore, managerial actions can lead to predictable outcomes;

- Second, many successful systems are driven by negative feedback processes toward predictable states of adaptation to the environment;

- Third, the dynamics of success are assumed to be a tendency toward equilibrium and thus stability, regularity and most of all predictability.

The role of management that underlies these approaches to change rests on a series of assumptions that may not be immediately obvious. Based on the assumption that success is dependent on the maintenance of equilibrium and stability, a management role often seen to be key is that of neutralizing external disturbances (Cyert and March, 1963), (Thompson, 1967). In line with the assumption that there is some degree of predictability to environmental change, a similar view argues that an important role of management consists of tracking and adjusting to the environment (Burns and Stalker, 1961); (Chandler, 1962); (Lawrence and Lorsch, 1967). In the faster-moving, more turbulent environment of the eighties, a more radical role was envisaged for managers. Miller and Friesen (1984) spoke of the need for management to make quantum leaps to adjust to change in structural gestalts. Moving away from earlier rational approaches to strategy making, Mintzberg (1987) saw management's role as crafting ad hoc strategies based on changing conditions. And in a decade where organizational change rose high on the management agenda, the mastery of change became central to the manager's role. Pettigrew (1987) stresses the need to take into account not just the content of the chosen strategy - the what - and the management of the process of change - the how - but also the inner and outer context for the change -

the why. Southern (1994) identifies two appropriate managerial responses to the need for change: technologically-oriented "systems intervention" and psychologically-oriented "organizational development." Underlying all these approaches however, is a deep belief that management interventions will cause predictable outcomes, and that the organization will emerge from its change process re-aligned with an environment that has remained static until the transformation is complete.

A key problem with efforts that aim to motivate change is that their impact is difficult to evaluate. Robert Ecles and Nitin Nohria decry the proliferation of massive organizational change programs with themes like "empowerment" and "culture." The reality is that none of these programs have produced proven results - although management consultants eagerly promote them. According to Ecles and Nohria's assessment, they are little more than feel-good exercises for management to make them feel that they are doing something right and useful for their firms.

How many **feel-good** strategic planning exercises have you participated in during the last ten years ?

It's the strategic process that provides the value-added. Not the final document. It's not the breath, but the **breathing** that we need.

If we are to gain new insights at the level of managerial practice, we have to identify and pursue a distinct line of thought resting on a different set of assumptions. Complex adaptive systems theory contains underlying assumptions quite different from the more Newtonian change literature. In a complex, fast-moving economy where cause-effect relationships are blurred, there is no predictability. Change cannot be driven, it can only be influenced when it emerges. And an important role of management is to sense and monitor emerging conditions, and to shape the evolution of events.

The complex adaptive systems paradigm also promises potential to provide that much-needed metric for measuring the impact of managerial interventions Roger Lewin et al (1993) propose that complexity theory based simulations can be powerful managerial tools. The key is to design simulations that incorporate the kinds of interpersonal exchanges that drive organizational performance. When this is possible, the relationships between parameter characteristics and system-wide behavior can be tested, and such simulations can be a proving ground for what has so far been management's least well understood efforts.

At the **heart** of all strategies are some basic assumptions. Strategic planners assume that management can make growth as one builds a house or a machine. The resulting models lead to the formulation of strategic plans that totally **ignore** human behavior and the changing environment.

Underlying Key Differences in Assumptions

Clearly Defined Goals
Change can be Controlled and Managed
Clear Connection between Cause and Effect
Management using Negative Feedback Loops
Success is achieved when Equilibrium and Stability is achieved
Management Key Role is Efficiency

⬇

Continuous Bifurcation
Change can only be Influenced when it Emerges
Perpetual Innovation and Organization
Operating at the Edge of Chaos
Attention to Initial Conditions and Emerging Events
Management Key Role is Monitoring System Feedback

Chapter 3

exploring the

roots of

strategy

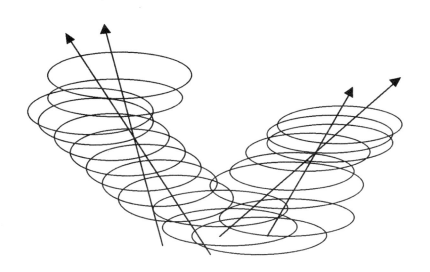

Exploring the roots of strategy

Central to the managerial frame is a conceptualization of what is "strategy". In strategy theory and practice, three main themes predominate.

- First is the notion of "fit" between the firm and its competitive environment. Fit entails the positioning of the firm vis-à-vis competitors, customers, suppliers and other external factors, plus the balancing of opportunities and resources.

- Second is the notion of "selectivity" in resource allocation - given a limited pool of resources, firms need to decide where and how resources should be allocated in order in maximize value appropriation or creation in the long run. In particular, the concept of corporate strategy centers around the problems of allocating resources, financial and otherwise, among competing investment alternatives.

- Third is the idea that strategy should be long-term. For many managers, any strategic investment means a willingness to take a long view rather than focus on immediate returns. A strategic move is one that has a distant payout and demands patient money.

It certainly goes without saying that every firm must ultimately effect a fit between its resources and the opportunities it pursues, that resource allocation is a strategic task, and that the firm must often countenance risk and uncertainty in the pursuit of strategic objectives or goals. But today the very structure of the firm's world is undergoing cascade changes and I argue that strategy in the face of complex foresight horizons should consist of an on-going set of practices that interpret and construct the relationship that make up the world in which the firm acts.

Again what is "strategy"? Once upon a time, almost everyone knew the answer to this. A strategy specified a pre-commitment to a particular course of action. Choosing a strategy meant optimizing among a set of specified alternatives or options, on the basis of an evaluation of the value and the probability of their possible consequences and outcomes.

Nearly all top business schools around the world produced generations of MBAs with tools in optimizing techniques, and strategic planning departments honed these tools to fit a myriad of particular circumstances: Harvard Business School's "Competition and Strategy" is an integrative course that takes a broad view of the firm's environment and adopts the perspective of the firm as a whole, drawing together ideas in several disciplines such as marketing, TQM, and finance. It demands mastery of several analytical tools and integrates them into an overall competitive strategy that creates competitive advantage. Second year courses include "Corporate Strategy," covering the creation of economic value, identification and leveraging of critical resources, and organization mechanisms necessary to achieve operating synergies; "Strategy, Commitment and Choice," which takes the perspective of a general manager developing strategy for a specific line of business, and also introduces concepts with respect to changes in strategic direction; and "Technology and Competitive Strategy." which develops skills in the systematic analysis of technological change as a major force influencing industry structure and patterns of competition. In short, strategy is about making a set of choices. As Michael Porter puts it, "at general management's core is strategy: defining a company's position, making trade-off, and forging fit among activities." There is a heavy emphasis on "fit" - one of the oldest ideas in strategy and one which Porter believes drives both competitive advantage and sustainability. Although "fit" is gradually being supplanted on the management agenda as managers turn away from the view of the company as a whole and focus on "core competencies," and "critical resources," Porter continues to view "fit" as a far more central component of competitive advantage that most managers realize.

> Look at managers and executives around you. Is optimizing pre-commitment still their **everyday** priority?

And for a long while, strategy as optimizing pre-commitment was a growth industry. But this approach is falling into disfavor because we all know that optimizing pre-commitment only makes sense when the future is known and the firm can foresee the likely consequences of its decisions. The reality foresight horizons are not always so clear and predictable. And as a result, an essential ingredient of strategy in the face of complicated foresight horizons becomes the organization of processes of exploration and adaptation.

> Do you have any processes in your organization for both continuous **exploration** and **adaptation**?

The field of strategy began with two parallel traditions starting in the 1960s with two different schools of thought. The first originated in the early work of Ken Andrews, C. Roland Christensen and others at Harvard Business School, and focused on the uniqueness of the individual organization. The other came from the work of Boston Consulting Group whose theory was built around the concept of the experience curve.

The first school viewed strategy as inherently situational, with each organization, each industry, and each market facing a different scenario. Therefore their approach encompassed a broad and general description with the bulk of necessary analysis geared uniquely to an individual case and situation. The underlying basic concept was that any successful firm will need to match its capabilities with the market needs - an idea of "fit" is here. Their framework attempted to be holistic, encompassing multiple dimensions of a firm and the existing environment including the firm's capabilities, the industry dynamics, and the managers' core values and competencies.

The Boston Consulting Group's ideas were just the opposite. A little background on this very interesting company which is also one of the most innovative consulting firms: The founder, Bruce Henderson, started his career in Westinghouse, later joined Arthur D. Little, but soon discovered his ideas were too racy for the firm and decided to leave. He started his consulting career in the trust department of a bank as a one-man consulting firm. He was certainly a revolutionary; "Consultants News" described him as, "like a medicine man in a room full of funeral directors." Henderson did not think that company should rely on economic growth and instincts to increase profits, rather that corporations needed a long-term strategy to sustain growth, particularly as growth started to taper in the late 1950s. Under Henderson's logic, the firm developed a strategy approach with insights about the very nature of profitability and competition in the market place. They wondered why companies with virtually identical manufacturing plants and equipment would have widely different costs. Their idea simply proposed that there was only one universal market dynamic on which all strategy should be based: the experience curve. They did not exactly invent the phenomenon, but capitalized on the insights and knowledge which were revolutionary at the time. They suggested that competitive advantage was defined basically by one single variable factor: cost. And cost depended on how fast a company could benefit from its experience as a result of the learning process, and thus in how fast it could gain market share advantage. So a firm's strategy was actually based on gaining market share. This concept later gave rise to another framework - the growth share matrix which was widely used by managers in the 1980s.

The two schools presented exactly opposite ideas; one suggested that each situation is unique and the other proposed a "one size fits all" solution. Then came Michael Porter with his five-forces theory. The starting point of his theory is that strategy must reflect two elements - industry structure and a company's relative position in the industry. No one will argue that the five-forces model has been one of the most useful and used tools in business as well as the most widely taught in business schools. Porter's books "Competitive Strategy" (1980) and "Competitive Advantage" (1985), can be found on every manager's bookshelf and are a must-read for MBAs.

Porter's "Five Forces" Model

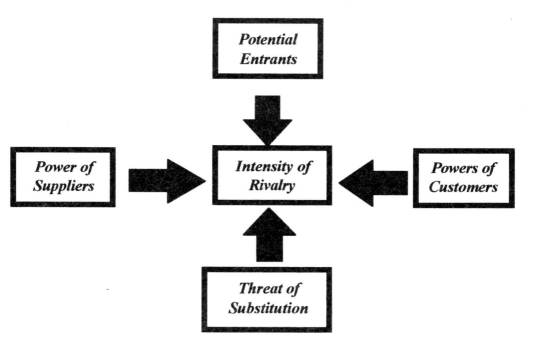

This is the point at which strategy began to emerge as a field of its own and was offered as a core course in business schools.

Porter's value chain analysis is still extremely useful today to help managers understand their business systems. Its key concept is that a company's activities can be broken down to gain a better understanding of the cost structures. Activities that represent a significant or rapidly growing share of costs or assets, whose cost behavior differs in some way, or which are performed differently by a competitor in the industry should be separated out. For each activity the cost behavior will be determined by what Porter calls a cost driver. Some examples of cost drivers are:

- "Economies of Scale" where increased volume leads to greater efficiency, and "diseconomies of scale" where excessive volume can impair a company's ability to respond quickly to consumer needs;

- "Capacity Utilization" - a key element in industries with high fixed costs, where the utilization of capital is critical. The correct measure of efficiency is to examine over time to take into account cyclical fluctuations;

- "Inter-relationships" meaning ways in which a firm's business units can club together to exploit economies;

- "Deliberate Choices" such as keeping the product range small or targeting a selected market niche only.

Most strategy tools including Porter's five-forces analysis, value chains, cost curves, experience curves and the idea of sustainable competitive advantage, originated from ideas developed in the early 1950s in the field of theory known as industrial organization. They were heavily based on industry structural analysis, which was then based on microeconomics theory. Modern neoclassical microeconomics was founded in the late eighteen century by people such as William Stanley, Carl Menger and Leon Walras and later synthesized into a more coherent theory by Alfred Marshall. Trying to make economics more scientific, they had to borrow ideas and mathematical apparatus from the leading science of their time which was energy physics. Some twenty years later other scientists achieved breakthroughs in energy physics that paved way for thermodynamics. Then the early neoclassicists copied the mathematics of mid-nineteenth century energy physics equation by equation, translating then metaphorically into the economics concepts of today. Although microeconomics theory has undergone many changes over the last fifty years, the basic concepts and ideas developed by Alfred Marshall, Irving Fisher and other scientists still resonate very much in today's teachings of economics. This is the family tree of strategy; from early thermodynamics theory and microeconomics to five-forces analysis, the lineage still very much affects the way we approach strategy and competition both in real world and business schools' teaching today.

Recent advances in technology, deregulation and the globalization of markets have resulted in turbulence for many industries such as infocom, healthcare and biotech. For companies competing in these industries, the organization set or the number of competitive forces they face has dramatically expanded, and technological innovations have accelerated the rate of change. To cope with this resulting turbulence, a number of strategy concepts have emerged.

First is the Hamel and Prahalad approach, which argues that the role of strategy should not be to accommodate an existing industry structure but rather to change it. They see the role of competitive innovation as identifying the orthodoxy in the incumbents' strategy and redefining the terms of engagement to exploit this orthodoxy. Hamel also proposes a new strategy frame - from "fit" to "stretch." He believes the first essential element of a new strategy frame is an aspiration that creates, by design, a chasm between ambition and resources. Strategy is stretch, as well as fit. The notion of strategy as stretch also helps to bridge the gap between those who see strategy as a "grand plan," thought up by the "great minds," and those who see strategy as a pattern in a stream of incremental decisions. Strategy as stretch is strategy by design, in the sense that top management does possess a relatively clear view of the goal line. Strategy as stretch is strategy by incrementalism to the extent that top management cannot pre-determine a twenty-year plan for global leadership, and must challenge the organization to clear the path towards leadership step by step.

Hamel further suggests that managers need to bring in more outsiders to help set strategies. One example is PECO Energy, a utility based in eastern Pennsylvania, has installed computer kiosks around the company to allow employees to make suggestions on strategy easily. He recommends increasing the "genetic variety" of the firm by recruiting people from a variety of backgrounds – as Apple did by hiring artist and musicians to help design the first Mac and Microsoft did by hiring a former dancer in Broadway to run its Internet service.

Another approach is from Anderson Consulting, probably the most aggressive marketers of management consulting services in the world, being the first in the industry to aggressively advertise its services both on TV and in print, at a cost of over US$10 million. The classical nature of strategy consulting requires the consultant and the management team to look at observable facts and arrive at a set of assumptions about the future. The next step is to design a strategy to achieve it. People from McKinsey, Bain or Boston Consulting Group would first get the strategy right, then pass it on or pass it down to the technology people to work on it. Anderson's approach believes that there is heavy interdependence among various components of a business, and that technology-blind strategies passed down from the top are not the best way to go. Technology can become strategy. Strategy, people, technology and processes all play important and interlocking roles in the Andersen philosophy of strategy making. Companies simply cannot be technology-blind and so no strategy can be technology-blind. Anderson advocates that business can no longer focus only on cost-cutting; growing the business is going to be more critical over the long term. Using emerging technologies to expand business opportunities will be the key theme in the new century. In short, there is no strategy when you do not have a digital strategy in order to compete for the future.

The third approach is that of D'Aveni, a professor in business strategy at Amos Tuck School of Business. D'Aveni argues that Hamel and Prahalad's ideas of competitive innovation and competence leveraging are not sustainable in these present hyper-competitive environments. He proposes the "New 7S Framework" to deal with the fleeting nature of competitive advantage. In essence, strategy is about continuously changing the rules of the game even when a firm is successful and ahead of its competitors. He extends the Hamel and Prahalad notion of competitive innovation to a continual process rather than a one-time breakthrough. The primary driver of strategy is strategic soothsaying and the anticipation of future customer needs through a constant monitoring of stakeholder satisfaction. D'Aveni's approach has major limitations: It assumes that strategic soothsaying is possible; and that competitive battles can be won by the firm's own actions in four areas of competition: cost and quality, timing and know-how, strongholds and deep pockets. He believes that it is possible for a firm to continuously move from one advantage to another. In the real world, it is highly unusual for any one firm to achieve uninterrupted success in a truly turbulent environment. And almost all successes require the presence of favorable external circumstances. D'Aveni has, however, made an important contribution to our knowledge of strategy making: D'Aveni for the first time shows that no organization can build a competitive advantage that is really sustainable, and that all advantages will eventually erode. He proposes that all companies must actively disrupt their own competitive advantages as well as the advantages of their competitors.

> Can any organization build a competitive advantage that is really **sustainable**?

Chapter 4

Who needs a Strategy?

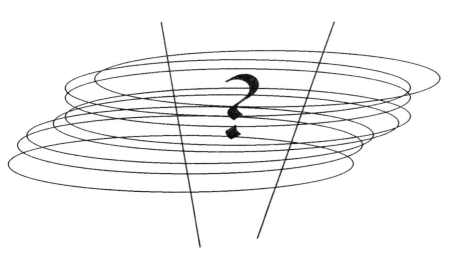

Who needs a strategy?

If we are to base our strategy making process on new assumptions, we first need to understand the assumptions that shape our existing approaches. In this chapter I explore the origins of the assumptions that underpin what we have come to know as strategy in the west, and contrast these with an alternative model.

When strategic planning first came about in the mid-1960s it was immediately embraced by corporate planners as the "one best way" to devise and implement strategies and enhance the competitiveness of business units. The whole idea was to separate the "planners" and the "implementers" or the "doers." Planners were supposed to produce a step-by-step guide for managers, who would then carry out the plan at the best of their abilities. According to the premise of strategic planning, life holds still while the planners work on a grand plan and the world awaits.

We know now of course that this is rather idealized. Ansoff (1965) wrote in his book "Corporate Strategy" that we shall refer to the period for which the firm is able to construct forecasts with an accuracy of plus or minus 20 % as the planning horizon of the firm. Can you imagine any company today that can forecast any planning horizon with any given accuracy?

Later management scholars saw quite a different role for strategic planners. Mintzberg (1994) suggested that planners should make their contribution around the strategy making process rather than inside it. They should be in a support mode to supply the hard and soft data that strategic planning requires. They should act as catalysts who support strategy making by encouraging managers to think strategically. Real strategic change requires inventing new categories and not rearranging old ones. Mintzberg suggested that the goal of those who promote planning was to reduce managers' power over strategy making.

Let us ask ourselves why, though, was the notion of strategic planning so readily accepted and adopted, particularly in the west? The main reasons lie in the heart of our mental logic - our "dominant logic" which, as defined by Bettis and Prahalad (1995) determines "the way in which managers conceptualize the business and make critical resource allocation decisions." The ability of human beings to assess a situation and design a response to tends to be limited by the capacity of the short-term working memory of our brains. As a result, we cope with the mass of information that constitutes reality by in effect ignoring most of it. We only select what we regard as most important and construct simple mental models of reality because it is probably the only way we can handle them. Over time we build up large number of such models based on past experience and apply them to simplify and new situations we encounter and design action in response. And when we work in groups, we often share our mental models. When we come to share the implicit models, we usually accept unquestioningly the even more hidden assumptions behind them. Collectively they become the dominant logic of the firm. The dominant logic continues to act as a filter for all information coming from the environment deemed to be irrelevant. These filtered data in turn become incorporated into the strategy, systems, values and expectations of the organization. The problem is, very often we mutually reinforce each other's models and assumptions when this may not be very appropriate.

For example, in IBM there was for years an assumption that mainframe computers were essential to the business, that industry conditions were quite stable, and more and more corporations would need to rely on mainframes for their needs. The dominant logic then became embedded in the strategy, reward systems and resource allocation systems, and persisted long after the circumstances which gave rise to it had changed. At one time, IBM's dominant logic in IBM's case was so persistent that it provoked a crisis which even threatened its existence. Almost the same thing happened to Apple computers; for years there was an assumption that proprietary systems and vertical manufacturing were essential to generate high margins, and that industry conditions were relatively stable, and that an increasing number of people would pay a premium for Apple's ease of use. Again the dominant persistent logic in Apple's case provoked a serious crisis which threatened Apple survival.

The dominant logic underpinning the notion of strategic planning is embodied in Alfred Sloan Jr.'s account of his work at General Motors and Alfred Chandler's concept of linking structure to strategy. In essence, a multi-national, multi-industries corporation needs to develop a systemic calculus to compare operations in different industries along common dimensions for coordination and also control. So the whole idea of strategic management became a matter of setting targets and objectives, budgeting resources, and comparing performance against forecasts. The BCG framework then became a handy tool for these purposes, and thus reinforced the dominant logic.

For an alternative approach, consider Japan in the early eighties. There were many instances where Japanese companies had no strategy as we know it; instead, they focused on executions and implementations. They did have grand visions and objectives but their strategic plans were often fuzzy, not written down, and in general based more on intuition than on hard data. In most cases, they imitated western market leaders, they were incremental, and most of all they placed themselves below the customer. And they did succeed, at least for a period of time: There were all kinds of stories documenting the huge successes of Japanese companies. Behind these successes lies a very different dominant logic.

To understand why the Japanese succeeded as intuitive incrementalists, we need first to reflect upon the meaning of strategy. In the west it means setting precise goals, measurable objectives into the future. For the Japanese, strategy is thinking long-term and is far more diffuse and imprecise, an allegiance to the longevity of the company and its people, rather than a well articulated objective. And it is that "vague" vision which many managers in the west find hard to understand: Andrew (1980), for example, referred to this sort of "muddling through" approach to strategy as "purposeless organizations". For managers trained in the western paradigm, the function of strategy is to make sure that all actions are geared to achieving the goal. There are "means/ends" chains linking actions to objectives. Managers are trained to keep their objective firmly view, chart a path to the top, calculate the effort required, and focus all efforts reaching the top - the approach called "strategic planning." The Japanese manager looks instead to the path itself, believing there will be a top to reach somewhere up there, but it cannot not quite be seen because of the cloud. Japanese managers take one step at a time, hurrying but slowly, and easily deal with obstacles in the path. In short, western managers and their Japanese counterparts have very different ideas about goals and how to reach them. This explains the quality orientation of many Japanese companies where "big-picture" oriented western managers filtered out minor deviations and improvised quick-fixes. The results were evident in the huge quality gap between Japanese and American automobiles in the 1980s automobile industry.

Traditional Strategic Planning Approach

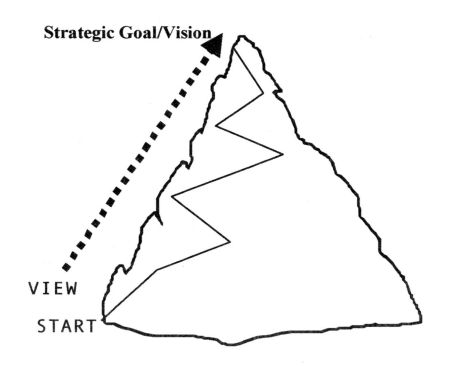

Japanese Strategy Approach

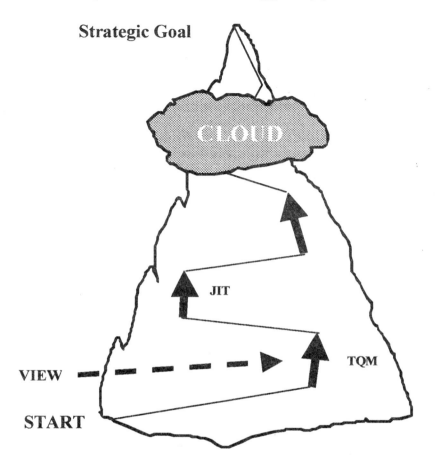

We need also to understand how the Japanese manager came to have this orientation towards implementation rather than strategy formulation. The answer is simple if we ask ourselves: When is strategy necessary? In general, strategy simply means some kind of premeditation before taking any action or committing any resource, or an evaluation of other available alternatives to achieve a goal. For the Japanese in the 1980s, few strategic choices were available. It is also true that the Japanese had little choice but to adopt imitation strategies then focus their energies on implementation. In the last few years, of course, there has arisen a much greater need for Japanese companies to have alternative strategies.

I must stress that is not my intention here to dismiss strategic planning or indeed advocate any approach over another. I am not proposing that we do not need strategy, or clear strategies. There are plenty of organizations who suffer from lack of articulated strategy and are therefore unable to mobilize their resources effectively and efficiently. We have seen many cases of companies that innovate piecemeal, producing a hodgepodge of inventions and technologies that collectively end up as less than the sum of their parts. Under certain stable conditions and when companies are in some form of crisis, it takes strong strategic visions and forceful leadership to bring them out of current situations.

I do believe, however, that the role of strategy formulation is dangerously overplayed. Our dominant logic makes us comfortable with the generalized principles and rational approach - hence the number of management consulting firms whose business is strategy formulation. There are far fewer successful consultants working with implementation. Why? Implementation requires an in-depth understanding of the context in which strategy is to be executed, and does not lend itself easily to a treatment in terms of principles.

Strategies do not emerge casually on convenient schedules or in a few brainstorming sessions. For many managers, strategic planning implies that they have control over something which is inherently uncontrollable. Strategy should not be about predicting the future – which is unpredictable by definition – but about the devising methods and systems for handling the unexpected when it happens.

> Strategy should not be about predicting the future – which is **unpredictable** by definition – but about the devising methods and systems for handling the **unexpected** when it happens.

Chapter 5

the heart of strategy:

the equilibrium systems

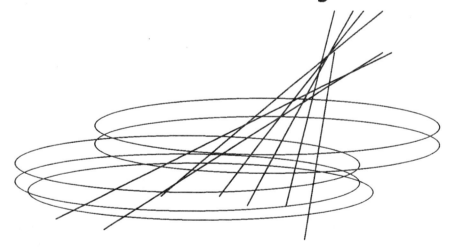

The heart of strategy: the equilibrium systems

Physicists, chemists as well as many biologists are all familiar with the two forms by which order arises. The first is known as low-energy equilibrium systems and can be explained with a simple example. Imagine a ball in a bowl that rolls to the bottom and stops. Its kinetic energy of motion, acquired because of gravity, has been dissipated into heat by friction. If there is no other energy or mass entering or leaving the bowl, that is, meaning the system is closed, the ball will then sit in equilibrium at the bottom of the bowl and remain static there. Similar examples exist in biology: Viruses are complex molecular systems of DNA or RNA molecular strands that form a core around which a variety of proteins assemble to form tail fibers, head structures etc. In a favorable environment, the viral particle self-assembles from its DNA or RNA and protein constituents, looking for a state of lowest energy, similar to the ball in the bowl case. Once a virus is formed, no other input of energy is required to maintain it.

In economic terms, the sides or the shape of the bowl represent the structure of a market, and the gravity that pulls the ball to it lowest energy state represents profit-seeking behavior pulling firms to their highest profit state. Provided we know the economic forces at work, and if all firms behave rationally, we can predict where the ball will come to a still in the bowl. This is when the prices, the quantities of goods produced and the profitability of firms are in equilibrium. If some external shock hits the system, the sides of the bowl may change shape and the ball will roll to a new point of equilibrium. This whole sequence of equilibrium - change a variable - new equilibrium is what economists call comparative statics, and forms the underpinning of

Alfred Marshall's economics and most business strategy. In a typical strategy, a firm will look at its position in the current industry structure, consider the shocks and changes that are occurring or might occur, and then develop a point of view on how the industry is likely to change and what that will mean for its own strategy. This approach makes three very important assumptions: that the industry structure is known, that diminishing returns apply, and that all firms are perfectly rational.

> Do you really think you **know** your industry structure?
>
> Does the law of diminishing returns **apply** in your case?
>
> Do you believe that all firms **act** rationally?

But just imagine what will really happen if rapid technological or strategic innovation makes producer costs and consumer preferences uncertain? What if firms lack complete information or different firms look at same information but with different interpretations, which happens all the time? What if we face not diminishing returns but increasing returns, which is happening more and more in this network economy? In traditional economics, the principle is that as production expands, every individual producer will eventually find that his costs per unit will start to rise because of a variety of reasons, and at some point size breeds inefficiency. The result is that firms stop growing and competition can flourish. Production of software does not appear to obey this rule, at least in a straightforward way. Once software has been written, it costs next to nothing to manufacture and market. That is the reason why some companies choose to sell their software very cheaply or even give it away for free. Once market share is established, it will be easier to sell follow-on or up-grade versions at higher prices. The law of increasing returns has other implications too; in the software industry, in addition to high development costs and low to zero production costs, network users want compatible software, and once they have chosen a particular software, they tend to "groove-in". The result will be winner takes all since network effects and customer "grove-in" will start a vicious circle of dominance. This concept extends far beyond the software industry into almost any information-based industry. The same can be said for on-line banking, insurance processing, news service, digital communications etc. Whenever computers and networks can greatly diminish variable costs, volume becomes all important. In these industries, the only strategy is "get big fast."

Get big **fast**!

If all the fundamental assumptions or rules underlying the equilibrium model are relaxed, the effect of the ball in the bowl will be much more dramatic. The sides of the bowl will begin to bend and flex, losing their smooth shape and becoming a landscape of hills or sand dunes or valleys, and there is no way to tell which side is up or down. Now it is almost impossible to predict where the ball will roll or stop, and Alfred Marshall loses his equilibrium. This is not pure theory, this is real since the ball in the bowl equilibrium model is the basis for all our strategy concepts. If we continue using our old ways of thinking to describe our current situations we get nothing more than "orthodox experiments disclosing orthodox novelty." This is what closed system produced – more of the same thing. We would like to clothe this orthodox novelty in the trappings of the new, but unfortunately the system does not work this way. As will become more evident in the chapters that follow, to be innovative and to escape velocity, companies must step outside their outmoded perspectives and reevaluate their mental models.

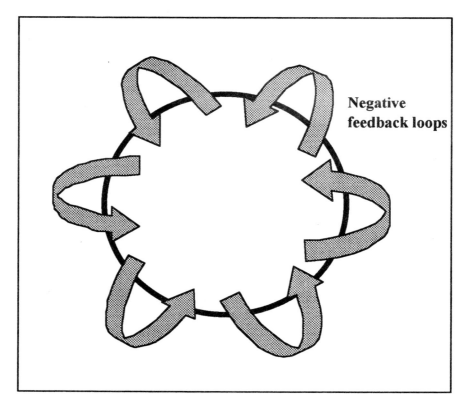

Negative feedback loops

Non-equilibrium ordered systems are sustained by the persistent dissipation of energy and matter, and so were named dissipative structures by the Nobel laureate Ilya Prigogine a few decades ago. These systems are in contrast to equilibrium thermodynamic systems where equilibrium is usually associated with collapse to the most probable, least ordered states. In dissipative systems, the flux of matter and energy through the system is the driving force generating order. Kauffman makes a distinction between viruses and free-living systems. Viruses are free living entities and need cells to reproduce. All living entities consist of cells, and cells are not low-energy structures. Cells are in fact non-equilibrium dissipative structures, and for most of them, equilibrium means death.

Alfred Marshall's model was a reasonable approximation to the manufacturing economy during his time and is still useful today in some industries. But it runs into deep trouble in today's dynamic high technology and service dominated economies. Let's consider a firm who wants to invest in entering a market as a new entrant. It faces dominant players that possess strong competitive advantages such as scale and brands, and that already compete fiercely with each other. Moreover, its own value proposition, while distinct from competitors', can easily be copied. In short, the entrant has no obvious source of sustainable competitive advantage. Any managers using the traditional strategy tools will surely not approve this investment. But what about companies like Dell Computer, Ikea, Virgin Atlantic Airways, Amazon.com, CNN, Southwest Airlines, eBay, and Hotmail.com. All these companies succeeded in spite of what the traditional model of strategy would perceive as long odds. They all violated the closed-equilibrium assumptions at the heart of this model. Their strategic innovations took advantage of increasing returns dynamics and their dominant logics were radically different from their incumbent competitors. It is easy to use traditional strategy frameworks to explain the success of these companies retrospectively, but it is much harder to use them to look forward in industries that are going through rapid and constant change. Conventional theory assumes that the world is predictable and relatively stable, and events can be explained by causal links that can be measured and monitored. Once we know what works and what not, we can then use it to good effect.

> Can you **explain** the success of companies like Dell, eBay, Amazon.com, CNN, Yahoo or Southwest using the framework of industry structure analysis?

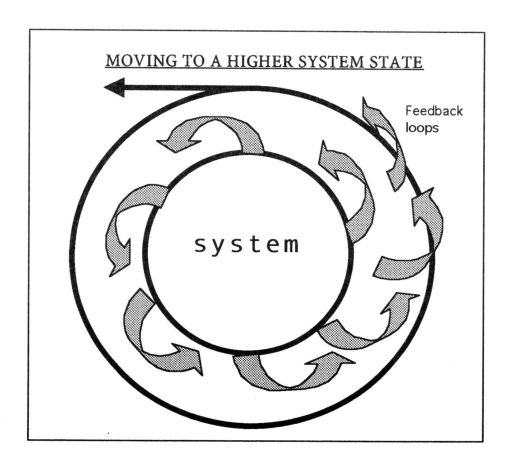

Traditional economics also contains implicit assumptions about the nature of organizations and the role of management. If the world we live in, or the world of organizations, is made up of machines composed of different parts, then management's job is to control and oil the machine keeping the parts going; as long as the machine works we can assume what it will produce and how it will do it. Thus, managers are really organizational maintenance engineers: whenever the machines break down, or organizational fires break out, managers will try to resolve the problem. That is, they only act when things gone wrong, so the feedback system is mostly negative.

But what if organizations are more like forests and gardens, rather than machines. Then much of what is happening is beyond the gardener's control in a far more radical sense. Gardeners have virtually no control over the weather, which is a chaotic system whose predication is difficult. Yet although it is chaotic, this does not mean that gardeners are impotent. On the contrary, it means they have to manage their gardens in a much more fluid way; for example they plant seeds only after certain conditions, then thin out plants only after they have grown. Despite the instability of weather systems, there are regular patterns underlying it. For example, weather has a consistency of temporal change which is known as seasons. No single day's weather can be accurately predictable but we can be fairly certain that most days in February will be quite cold, at least in Boston. This regularity underlying the irregular dynamic is referred to as a "strange attractor" - it appears to set limits on the degree of chaos over time and to pull the extremes back closer to norm. At the level of human beings this means that while any individual may appear to be random and chaotic, this does not mean that the activities of the group as a whole are consequently random and chaotic. On the contrary, to pick another example from nature, although the activities of the watch ant may appear random, the overall result is an extremely powerful social organization of ants. The reality is that many social systems are anything but machine-like; we simply have the wrong metaphor, because social systems' are integrative recursive systems that can exhibit discontinuous change over time.

Do you treat your organization like a **machine** or more like a **garden**?

In these circumstances, strategy tools such as Porter's five-forces analysis may offer little help especially to industries such as biotech, life sciences, telecom where there is profound technical change, industry convergence, globalization and increasing returns in sectors such as the Internet. They can only produce a "snapshot" analysis of the industry . Analyzing causal links within complex systems becomes critically impossible because of the chaotic relationships that exist and the way that initial conditions generate potentially large and unpredictable variants through time - we simply cannot trace the relationship between the butterfly's wings and the storm, and it is the relationships, not the things in themselves, that are critical.

What managers need today is a model of a world where innovation, change and uncertainty, rather than equilibrium are the natural state of things. There are already many indications that market can be viewed as inherently dynamic rather than a static system. When adaptive agents interact in a web of relationships, evolutionary changes in one agent will affect the evolution of others. This co-evolution is seen in economics when an innovation such as the Internet produces ripple effects throughout the whole economy - the development of routers, high speed modems, fiber optics cable, browsers and other security and networking software.

Today we need a model of a world where **innovation**, **change** and **uncertainty** rather equilibrium are the natural state of things.

Traditional economics has never been able to explain innovation and growth, except perhaps as the result of random exogenous shocks from technology. A new economics based on complexity will help us gain insights into the endogenous evolutionary forces that drive Schumpeter's waves of "creative destruction" through the economy. Not only will that the substance of economics be transformed, but so will all the research techniques. Traditional economics uses mostly mathematical proofs to model its theories. The benefit of this is that one can be confident about the logical rigor of the result. The problem is that it restricts you to rather simple assumptions that do not necessarily reflect the ways things work in the real world; and if the assumptions do not reflect the real world, all results will be irrelevant. The new economics will need to turn to powerful computers with sophisticated simulations based on more realistic assumptions. In agent-based models, for example, a company can be modeled as an intelligent computer program that is capable of learning and adapting. You can put a bunch of these programs into a simulated competitive environment, unleash the forces of evolution and monitor the evolutionary process. These systems cannot predict the precise changes, which in complex systems are almost impossible to forecast, but they will be useful in fostering insights into how and why markets behave in any particular fashion. Such modeling is possible today, although most models are still work in process only.

Developing strategies based on just **narrow predictions** about the future is entirely the wrong mind-set for an inherently **uncertainty** world.

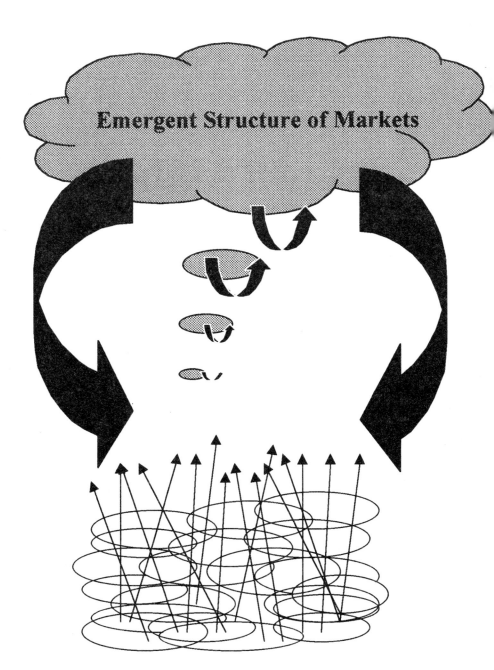

Chapter 6

The new science of complexity theory

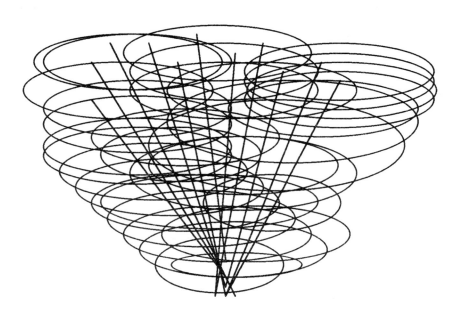

The new science of complexity

The field of "complexity" has blossomed in the last few years attracting the attention of researchers in physics, biology, mathematics, computer science and economics. It has recently begun to generate strong interest among management academics and practitioners. In management, there is always a danger of "faddism" taking over before the implications which "complexity theory" holds for the discipline have been properly digested. Through this book, I hope to be able to help managers diagnose the conditions in which a complexity theory approach is appropriate to their strategy making process, and to provide a practical strategy making tool.

The science of complexity represents an attempt to understand dynamic systems phenomena which had previously been overlooked by more traditional branches of science. In its modern usage, "complexity" can be defined as the quantity of regularities or patterns that can be observed in a body of information. That is, while patterns in both completely random and completely ordered information can be described using very few statements, in the zone between order and disorder, many regularities can be observed and described. In this zone, the degree of effective "complexity" is significant. I am personally very convinced that any nations, organizations or individuals who can master the new science of complexity will become the cultural, economic and political superpowers of the next century. Up to this date, there's really only a handful of active practitioners and complexity is still a new science that perhaps many people have never heard of. For one thing the only way to understand complex systems is to use computers, because such systems are all highly non-linear and beyond all standard mathematical analysis.

Order arises out of a complex dynamic system as global properties flow from aggregate behavior of individuals. In an ecosystem, the interaction of species within the community might confer a degree of stability on it. In many cases, stability in this context would be an emergent property. In industrial societies, the aggregate behavior of companies, consumers and financial markets produce the modern capitalist economies. They all act as if they are guided by an invisible hand.

Systems exhibiting such complexity are referred to as "complex systems", and they fall into two categories: complete deterministic systems and complex adaptive systems. Complete deterministic systems tend to be physical systems with constant parameters, and their study is generally referred to as chaos theory (Lorenz, 1963; Nicolis and Prigogine, 1977). Lorenz describes these systems as "a restricted set of phenomena that evolve in predictably unpredictable ways." Examples could include patterns of smoke rising, or the formation of snowflakes. Complex adaptive systems are probabilistic rather than deterministic, and include agents or lower-scale systems which interact, learn and modify their behavior over time. Factors such as non-linearity and positive feedback can magnify apparently insignificant differences in initial conditions to lead to huge consequences, meaning that long-term outcomes for complex adaptive systems are unknowable. Like many social science researchers, I believe adaptive rather than deterministic systems have more immediate implications for organizations.

Much of the research on complex systems in biology has focused on the use of cellular automata. Jon von Neuman, the brilliant Hungarian mathematician, invented cellular automata in the 1950s, during his quest for self-reproducing machines. Cellular automata, the computer jock's equivalent of a menagerie, is a kind of complex dynamic system. Just picture an infinitely larger grid of squares, like endless graph paper rolled out on a football stadium. Each of the cells or tiny squares may either be black or white, depending on activity of the cells next to it. Simple rules govern the state of each cell, such as if four or more of a cell's contiguous eight cells are black then the one in the middle changes state. Each cell reacts according to the activities of the cell surrounding it. Complex dynamic patterns develop and roam across the entire grid, the nature of which is influenced but not tightly determined in detail according to the activity rules.

The rule is simple and the state of a single cell is determined, via a set of rules, by the state(s) of its immediate neighbors (often in one-, two- or three-dimensional space). States are designated as "on" or "off" or perhaps or "dead." The Game of Life, a simple computer program that was once popular among microcomputer buffs in the mid-1980s, is a well-known form of cellular automata. Researchers have been concerned with the emergent behavior of the system; the consistent patterns that emerge from the interaction of many elements under different rule sets.

There are basically four classes of behavior that are identified in cellular automata:

- In Class I models, any combination of live and dead cells quickly approaches a steady equilibrium state where all cells are "dead." Thus, life is extinguished.

- In Class II models, the cells develop into static groupings or patterns of live cells, or perhaps groups of cells that oscillate between fixed states.

- Class III models are the opposite of Class I and II models. Class III models are indeed chaotic - the cells alternate wildly between 'on' and 'off' positions and there are simply no predictable patterns or stability.

- The final set of models, Class IV, are a combination of Class II and III "...coherent structures that propagated, grew, split apart, and recombined in a new wonderfully complex way." Class IV models are capable of producing "extended transients" such as the Game of Life's gliders: structures that can survive and propagate for an arbitrarily long time. To a greater or lesser extent the behavior of these extended transients appears to be stable and predictable. However, there is also a degree of uncertainty in Class IV systems, and extended transients may be destroyed by an interaction with another "entity" or completely random "mutation." In the Game of Life, one mutation in the wrong place can destroy an extended transient almost instantly.

There is a growing body of evidence in physics and biology, that complex systems tend to evolve to a state of complexity at the edge of chaos (i.e. into Class IV systems). Studies on phenomena as disparate as sand piles, earthquakes and artificial life have found that systems move towards complexity or Class IV behavior. Class IV behavior enables entities in the system to maximize the benefits of stability while retaining a capacity to change. Some observers from outside the pure natural sciences, including Waldrop (1992) and Stacey (1996) also make reference to the notion of "edge of chaos," where the system is balanced between stability and anarchy, a state in which spontaneous self-organization, adaptation and "creativity" is believed to flourish.

System	Order	Chaos	Randomness
Paradigm	Clocks, Planets	Clouds, Weather	Snow on TV Screen
Predictability	High	Short-Term	None
Effect of Small Errors	Very Small	Explosive	None Just Errors
Dimension	Finite	Low	Infinite
Strange Attractor	Easy	Tricky	Poor
Control	Cycle, Point	Strange Fractal	No

Scientists have explored the probability of change occurring in complex systems at the edge of chaos. A large number of phenomena seem to follow a power-law distribution. In this distribution, for every one event of size 1000 (in any scale), 1000 events of size one will occur. This has led to the theory of "punctuated equilibrium." which states that change in any complex system at the edge of chaos will tend to be small most of the time, but occasionally a large scale change will occur.

An example of punctuated equilibrium

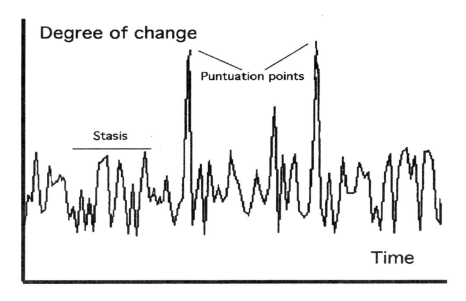

Change in any complex system will tend to be small most of the time, but occasionally a **large** scale change will occur.

As the level of turbulence in the system increases, the life expectancy of an extended transient (a company/firm/organization) will decline. Thus with increasing turbulence, Class IV "complexity" systems will move away from a resemblance to Class II "stable" systems and towards the characteristics of a Class III "chaos" system. This is not to say, however, that increasing turbulence will tend to propel systems into chaos. Recall that in the power-law distribution small shocks to the system are much more numerous than large shocks. These shocks are just as likely to make the system less turbulent as more turbulent, resulting in a pulling back from the edge of chaos and a move towards stability.

The interest in complex adaptive systems research has accelerated over the past twenty years, with centers for their study now in existence at many prestigious institutions around the world. Notable among these is the Santa Fe Institute in the southwest United States, founded in 1984. This institution brings together such thinkers on the subject as Nobel laureates Murray Gell-Mann, Phil Anderson and Kenneth Arrow, along with authorities such as John Holland, Stuart Kauffman, and Brian Arthur. Representing a range of disciplines including physics, biology, computer science and economics, these scientists are together attempting to shed new light on the economy, human society, artificial life and ecology as complex adaptive systems.

Ongoing research conducted at the Santa Fe Institute has resulted in complex adaptive systems phenomena being defined with increasing precision . Although to date no universally accepted definition exists, since the availability of super computing power and advanced mathematics, scientists have been able to discover that the complex adaptive systems are governed by some deep common laws. These laws can eventually help us develop new insights into daily problems ranging from traffic jams in Tokyo, to the evolution of the virus, to the volatility of the currencies market. A good number of economists are fully convinced that economies are complex adaptive systems, rather than the closed equilibrium systems that they all previously assumed. Though the case has yet to be proven and argued, research conducted by many eminent economists, notably Kenneth Arrow and Brian Arthur of the Santa Fe Institute, is strongly supportive.

John Holland of the University of Michigan and the Santa Fe Institute is one of the early researchers whose complexity theories invention has real practical applications. He is also the inventor of genetic algorithm which has achieved very impressive results. Holland identifies four main properties of complex adaptive systems:

- Aggregation: complex adaptive systems can be grouped into categories, which can then be nested into larger aggregates. For example, a human being is a complex adaptive system, but also acts as an agent in a larger complex adaptive system (an organization), which forms part of a still larger complex adaptive system (the economy), and so on.

- Non-Linearity: a given action can lead to several possible outcomes, some of which are disproportionate in size to the action itself. The "whole" is therefore not equal to the sum of the "parts".

- Flows: the agents of complex adaptive systems are connected by networks and nodes. The "flows" can give rise to two important phenomena: "multiplier effects" which occur through the interlined system, and "recycling effects."

- Diversity: the persistence of any individual agent in a complex adaptive system depends on the context provided by the other agents in the system. Each agent occupies a "niche" which will be filled by other agents should that agent vanish.

Holland also complex adaptive systems by notes three mechanisms by which complex adaptive systems operate:

1. Tagging: the mechanism by which agents can distinguish boundaries among complex adaptive systems. Examples include national flags among countries, business cards among companies, and sweatshirts and backpacks with schools' names among business schools.

2. Internal Models: adaptive agents learn over time to anticipate some of the results of their actions. They do go through a set of decision rules they use to recognize patterns, make decisions, and adapt over time. These internal models are referred to as schema by many researchers.

3. Building Blocks: agents have the ability to decompose complex phenomena into parts, which can be assembled and reassembled in different ways to deal with everyday situations, or to improve internal models.

In a critique provided by Johnson and Burton (1994), concern was expressed regarding the difficulty of using complexity theory in organization science research given:

- Greater uncertainty in testing conclusions due to the generally smaller number of data points.

- A perceived over dependence on metaphoric use of the theories.

- The wholesale abandonment of Newtonian principles thought to lie behind much complexity research by organizational researchers.

It is not my intention in this book to completely dismiss the Newtonian framework, which works particularly well in many situations involving closed systems. Rather, I attempt to challenge the use of some of these assumptions in areas where we believe they are no longer appropriate, such as strategic management and organizational science. While I understand the concern expressed about the overuse of metaphor, Johnson and Burton concede that metaphors are "fair game" in the context of discovery. The value of analogies has similarly been highlighted by Holland: analogy helps generate new rules applicable to a novel target problem by transferring knowledge from a source domain that is better understood (Holland et al., 1986). Finally, it is not my intention to present complexity theory as an iron-clad "unified theory of everything." I just hope this book can shed some light on organizational adaptation by adopting complex adaptive systems as one of our theoretical lenses. This represents a "rethinking" distinction, as it identifies and replaces assumptions rather than refines what is already known in the change management area based on existing assumptions.

A new economics based on complex adaptive systems has not yet been discovered, and I believe it is still a bit too early to claim a new economic theory. However, the science of complexity emphasizes the importance of history as determining paths a system might take in the future, and the economy is much more path dependent and history dependent than earlier economists thought.

The changes wrought by the science of complexity are sweeping through macroeconomics. Its impact is most notable in the studies conducted on the role of expectations in interest rate fluctuation by Tom Sergeant and others. Paul Romer has done important work using complexity theory to examine the sources of economic growth, showing that growth leads to growth as an economy builds knowledge and invests in fixed costs. Paul Krugman has made excellent contributions in trade theory. In addition, antitrust theory is coming under new scrutiny with the findings of complexity theory. Antitrust policy was developed for diminishing returns industries. Firms that operate under the rules of increasing returns would have very different trust relationships. Antitrust theory must also take this into account.

The new economics will be based on a rather realistic model of cognitive behavior. Traditional economics assumes that all people are alike in their thinking processes and that they make choices as if they were solving complicated deductive equations that enabled them to make the best assumptions are an over simplifications, but then they were needed to create the ball in the bowl model. In the economy, positive feedback might be defined as the phenomenon of increasing returns. An increased knowledge base, for example, leads to greater economic growth. As knowledge becomes embedded in technology, economies experience increasing returns from the acquisition and investment of new knowledge. High technology industries are different from industries that experience diminishing returns in that the knowledge input, and usually the costs, are up front. As a result, in high technology industries, network effects accrue as technologies become standardized in the marketplace. As an economy becomes more high tech, it experiences deep sources of increasing returns promoting highly unstable competition. A company may learn by using a product and thus find that development and production must constantly adapt. In this unstable market, chance events can cause a product to lock-in around a standard, but lock-in may not be optimal. Increasing returns from lock-in can mean that countries may take over in certain industries, such as Japan in consumer electronics, or the US in aircraft. Cells within the economy can increase productivity, but under the paradigm of increasing returns, the ability of an agent to gain in productivity depends upon their willingness to invest in education. While many observers have noted the role of increasing returns in high technology industries over the years, until the advent of dynamic modeling and complexity theory, there has not been a way to model this phenomenon. There currently exists a rudimentary ability to analyze these phenomena with rigorous computer experiments.

Advanced computer simulations techniques and cognitive science now enable us to make much more realistic assumptions. Computer modeling, of course, is not new to business. Simulations of a different sort already have a well-established role in operations planning such as in factories and refineries. These are based on exact, deterministic equations. If the synthesis gas is entering the pressure vessel at x pounds per hour, ammonia is produced at a rate of y pounds. One gold mine in Papua New Guinea, for example, has an animated simulator that shows where all the trucks and excavators are located and what they are doing. Equation-based computer models, however, are inadequate to cope with complex, dynamic systems with a lot of interactions and an element of randomness—presently unpredictable things like record sales. That is where the virtual people, cities full of them, enter the picture. It helps, of course, since computation has gotten so cheap to a point that most powerful desktop computers can already perform this type of task. In the old days, complex simulations demanded Cray supercomputers easily costing a few million dollars. The Price Waterhouse Coopers music buyer simulation can execute one trillion machine instructions to do one simulation. It can be run on a $8,000 workstation.

The disaster recovery division of Comdisco, the Chicago-based lessor of mainframe computers and other electronic equipment, is designing an agent-based model using simulation software from Monterey, Calif.-based Thinking Tools Inc. The object is to make sure a corporate client can withstand disasters such as a massive computer outage. Agent-based models have a few ingredients in common. One ingredient, of course, is agents, usually a large population of them. A traffic model built for Dallas can handle 10 million drivers. The second ingredient is a set of rules that determine how these agents behave when they encounter one another. And the third ingredient present in almost all agent-based models is an element of chance. The probability that this particular driver on the west side of Santa Monica Highway will take Santa Monica Boulevard to work may be known in advance, but whether he or she in fact does is determined only when the program is run. The software rolls an electronic pair of dice for each driver. Computer model builders called this the Monte Carlo method. Ten years of urban development, determined by 300 cycles of the model, can now be compressed into just a few minutes of computing time

Chapter 7

the growth of
complexity

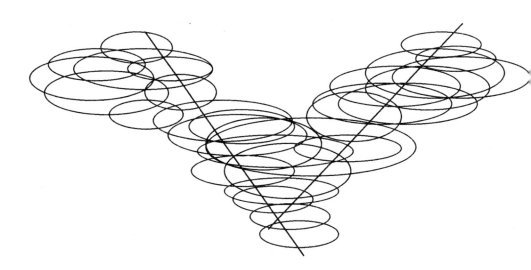

"The affinities of all the beings of the same class have sometimes been represented by a great tree. I believe this simile largely speaks the truth. The green and budding twigs may represent existing species; and those produced during each former year may represent the long succession of extinct species... The limbs divided into great branches, and these into lesser and lesser branches, were themselves once, when the tree was small, budding twigs; and this connection of the former and present buds by ramifying branches may well represent the classification of all extinct and living species in groups subordinate to groups... From the first growth of the tree, many a limb and branch has decayed and dropped off, and these lost branches of various sizes may represent those whole orders, families, and genera which have now no living representatives, and which are known to us only from having been found in a fossil state... As buds give rise by growth to fresh buds, and these, if vigorous, branch out and overtop on all a feebler branch, so by generation I believe it has been with the great Tree of Life, which fills with its dead and broken branches the crust of the earth, and covers the surface with its ever branching and beautiful ramifications"

Charles Darwin 1859

The growth of complexity

At least since the days of Darwin, evolution has been associated an increase in complexity. If we go back in time we see originally only simple systems (elementary particles, atoms, molecules, unicellular organisms) while more and more complex systems appear in later stages. To understand the principles behind growth in complexity, we must begin with evolutionary theory.

We see evolution as based on the trial-and-error process of variation and natural selection of systems at all levels of complexity. The term "natural selection" comes from the Darwinian theory of biological evolution, which distinguishes between "natural" and "artificial" selection, where specific features are retained or eliminated depending on a goal or intention. The "implicit goal" of natural selection is maintenance or reproduction of a configuration at some level of abstraction. The selection is natural in the sense that there is no actor or purposive system making the selection. The selection we are discussing is purely automatic or spontaneous, without any planning or design involved. Many criticisms have been and are still being levied against the Darwinian view of evolution and I will not discuss the on-going criticisms stating that there are designs or plans guiding evolution, but focus on a more recent upsurge of people, many of whom are associated with the systems movement, who state that natural selection must be complemented by self-organization in order to explain evolution. The narrow or specific interpretation of Darwinism sees evolution as the result of selection by the environment acting on a population of organisms competing for resources. The winners of the competitions, those who are most fit to gain the resources necessary for survival and reproduction, will be selected, and the others eliminated.

Even when abstracting from the fact that we are speaking about "organisms," this view of evolution entails basically two strong restrictions. First it assumes that there is a multitude ("population") of configurations undergoing selection, and secondly that selection is carried out by their common environment. However it simply cannot explain the evolution of a "population of one" as there is no need for competition between simultaneously present configurations. A configuration can be selected or eliminated independently of the presence of other configurations: a single system can pass through a sequence of configurations, some of which are retained while others are eliminated. The only "competition" involved is one between subsequent states of the same system. Such selection can still be "natural." More importantly this selection does not in any way presuppose the existence of an environment external to the configuration undergoing selection. It is easy enough to imagine configurations that are intrinsically stable or unstable. A cloud of gas molecules in a vacuum (i.e. an "empty" environment) will diffuse, independently of any outside forces. A crystal in the same vacuum will retain its rigid crystalline structure. The first configuration (the cloud) is eliminated, the second one maintains. The stability of the structure, functioning as a selection criterion, is purely internal to the configuration: no outside forces or pressures are necessary to explain them. In cases like these, the selection is inherent in the configuration itself, and an asymmetric transition from varying to stable may be called "self-organization." In the present view, "natural selection" encompasses both external, "Darwinian selection", and internal, "self-organizing" selection.

> "The American Beauty rose can be produced in take splendor and fragrance which bring cheer to his beholder by sacrificing the early buds which grow up around it. This is not an evil tendency. It is merely the working out of a law of nature and a law of God."
>
> J.D.Rockerfeller

From the point of view of classical evolutionary theory there is no a priori reason why more complicated systems would be preferred by natural selection. Evolution tends to increase fitness, but fitness can be achieved equally well by very complex as by very simple systems. For example, according to some theories, viruses, the simplest of living systems, are degenerate forms of what were initially much more complex organisms. Since viruses live as parasites, using the host organisms as an environment that provides all the resources they need to reproduce themselves, maintaining a metabolism and reproductory systems of their own is just a waste of resources. Eventually, natural selection will eliminate all superfluous structures, and thus partially decrease complexity.

The question of the why complexity of individual systems appears to increase so strongly during evolution can be easily answered by combining the traditional cybernetic idea of the "Law of Requisite Variety" and the co-evolutionary concept of the Red Queen Principle."

Ashby's Law of Requisite Variety states that in order to achieve complete control, the variety of actions a control system should be able to execute must be at least as great as the variety of environmental perturbations that need to be compensated. Evolutionary systems (organisms, societies, self-organizing processes ...) obviously would be fitter if they had greater control over their environments, because that would make it easier for them to survive and reproduce. Thus, evolution through natural selection would tend to increase control, and therefore internal variety. Since we may assume that the environment as a whole always has more variety than the system itself, the evolving system would never be able to achieve complete control, but it would at least be able to gather sufficient varieties to more or less control its most direct neighborhood. We might imagine a continuing process where the variety of an evolving system "A" slowly increases towards but never actually matches the infinite variety of the environment.

However, according to the complementary principles of selective variety and of requisite constraint, Ashby's law should be restricted in its scope: at a certain point further increases in variety diminish rather than increase the control that system "A" has over its environment. "A" will asymptotically reach a trade-off point, depending on the variety of perturbations in its environment, where requisite variety is in balance with requisite constraint. For viruses, the balance point will be characterized by a very low variety, for human beings by a very high one.

This analysis assumes that the environment is stable. However, the environment of "A" itself consists of evolutionary systems (say "B," "C," and "D") which are in general undergoing the same asymptotic increase of variety towards their trade-off points. Since "B" is in the environment of "A" and "A" in the environment of "B," the increase in variety in the one will create a higher need (trade-off point) in variety for the other, since it will now need to control a more complex environment. Thus, instead of an increase in complexity characterized by an asymptotic slowing down, we get a positive feedback process, where the increase in variety in one system creates a stronger need for variety increase in the other. The net result is that many evolutionary systems that are in direct interaction with each other will tend to grow more complex, and this with an ever increasing speed.

The present argument does not imply that all evolutionary systems will increase in complexity: those (like viruses, snails or mosses) that have reached a good trade-off point and are not confronted by an environment putting more complex demands on them will maintain their present level of complexity. But it suffices that some systems in the larger ecosystem are involved in the complexity race, to see an overall increase of available complexity.

As an example, in our present society, individuals and organizations tend to gather more knowledge and more resources, increasing the range of actions they can take, since this will allow them to cope better with the possible problems appearing in their environment. If the people you cooperate or compete with (e.g. colleagues, business partners) become more knowledgeable and resourceful, you too will have to become more knowledgeable and resourceful in order to respond to the challenges they pose to you. The result is an ever faster race towards more knowledge and better tools, creating the "information explosion" as we all know it.

During the early "Industrial Revolution," human beings "evolved" into "factory man" where on the shop floor and on assembly line their life was basically reduced to just one thing, one single function, like a single-purpose cell in a vast economic organism. Now the economic organism is evolving into something entirely different. But the organization is not responding at the same pace as the individual, and the tragedy is as that man or woman is becoming more complex, the higher organization is not liberating fast enough to cope with this, and societies are coming apart. I don't know whether we would rather be a single skin cell, but we are already more like paramecia.

Are we all currently involved in a complexity **race** resulting in an overall increase of available complexity?

Evolutionary biologist L. Van Halen proposed the phenomenon of the "Red Queen Principle" to describe increasing complexity in co-evolving systems. It is based on the observation to Alice by the Red Queen in Lewis Carroll's "Through the Looking Glass" that "in this place it takes all the running you can do, to keep in the same place." In evolution the principle says that for an evolutionary system, continuing development is needed just in order to maintain its (relative) fitness.

The most curious part of the thing was, that the trees and the other things around them never changed their place at all : however fast they went, they **never** seemed to pass anything. " I wonder if all the things are moving with us? " thought poor Alice.

Lewis Carroll   Through the Looking Glass

Since every improvement in one species will lead to a selective advantage for that species, variation will normally continuously lead to increases in fitness in one species or another. However, since in general different species are co-evolving, improvement in one species implies that it will get a competitive advantage over other species, and thus be able to capture a larger share of the resources available to all. This means that fitness increase in one evolutionary system will tend to lead to fitness decrease in another system. The only way that a species involved in a competition can maintain its fitness relative to the others is by in turn improving its design.

An obvious example of this effect are the "arms races" between predators and prey, where the only way predators can compensate for a better defense by the prey (e.g. rabbits running faster) is by developing a better offense (e.g. foxes running faster). In this case we might consider the relative improvements (running faster) to be also absolute improvements in fitness. However, this is not always the case. The example of trees shows that in some instances the net effect of an "arms race" may also be an absolute decrease in fitness. Trees in a forest are normally competing for access to sunlight. If one tree grows a little bit taller than its neighbors it can capture part of their sunlight. This forces the other trees in turn to grow taller, in order not to be overshadowed. The net effect is that all trees tend to become taller and taller, yet still gather on average just the same amount of sunlight, while spending much more resources in order to sustain their increased height. This is an example of the problem of suboptimization: optimizing access to sunlight for each individual tree does not lead to optimal performance for the forest as a whole.

The reasoning why individual systems will on average tend to increase in complexity can now be extended to show how the complexity of the environment as a whole increases. Let us consider a global system, consisting of a multitude of co-evolving subsystems. The typical example would be an ecosystem, where the subsystems are organisms belonging to different species. Now, it is already well-documented by ecologists and evolutionary biologists that ecosystems tend to become more complex. The number of different species increases, and the number of dependencies and other linkages between species increases. This has been observed over the geological history of the earth, as well as in specific cases such as island ecology where the island initially contains very few species, but where more and more arise through immigration or through the differentiation of a single species specializing in different niches. An example is Darwin's famous finches on the Galapagos Islands.

As is well explained by E.O. Wilson in his "The Diversity of Life", not only do ecosystems typically contain lots of niches that will eventually be filled by new species, there is also a self-reinforcing tendency to create new niches. Indeed, a hypothetical new species (let's call them "thing") occupying a hitherto empty niche, creates by its mere presence a set of new niches. Other different species can now specialize in somehow using the resources produced by that new species, e.g. as parasites that suck the thing's blood or live in its intestines, as predators that catch and eat things, as plants that grow on the thing's excrement, as furrowers that use abandoned things' holes, etc. etc. Each of these new species again creates new niches, that can give rise to even further species, and so on ad infinitum. These species all depend on each other: take the things away and dozens of other species may become extinct.

This principle is not limited to ecosystems or biological species: if in a global system (e.g. the interior of a star, the primordial soup containing different interacting chemicals, new kinds of viruses etc.) a stable system of a new type appears through evolution (e.g. a new element in a star, or new chemical compound), this will in general create a new environment or selector. This means that different variations will either adapt to the new system (and thus be selected) or not (and thus be eliminated). Elimination of unfit systems may decrease complexity, and selection of fit systems is an opportunity for increasing complexity, since it makes it possible for systems to appear which were not able to survive before. For example, the appearance of a new species creates an opportunity for the appearance of species-specific parasites or predators, but it may also cause the extinction of less fit competitors or prey.

However, in general the power for elimination of other systems will be limited in space, since the new system cannot immediately occupy all possible places where other systems exist. For example, the appearance of a particular molecule in a pool of "primordial soup" will not affect the survival of molecules in other pools. So, although some systems in the neighborhood of the new system may be eliminated, in general not all systems of that kind will disappear. The power for facilitating the appearance of new systems will similarly be limited to a neighborhood, but this does not change the fact that it increases the overall variety of systems existing in the global system. The net effect is the creation of a number of new local environments or neighborhoods containing different types of system, while other parts of the environment stay unchanged. The environment as a whole becomes more differentiated and, hence, increases its complexity.

The Santa Fe Institute's models based on research into the nature and functioning of complex adaptive systems, support the notion of increasing complexity. The Santa Fe models see the living world as co-evolving, co-emerging, mutually interdependent elements and forces that operate at different levels. Each element that we choose to focus on is influenced dynamically by higher levels and by constituent lower levels. Key distinctions for understanding this nature are that the elements are largely autonomous and are connected or organized in particular ways. Each autonomous agent has various schemas or strategies, all seen as having information processing entities as their key basis of organization. Each increase in complexity creates the opportunity for even more complexity in "spirals of innovation." By increasing complexity in the world, we are actually saying the number of relationships of interdependence is expanding. As Kauffman says, there are increasingly numerous ways to "get lunch."

There are many different kinds of complex adaptive systems; the nature ecosystem including the oceans and forests, the human immune system, the financial markets, and the traffic on the streets. All of these are open systems comprising a large number of agents whose dynamic interactions and self-organizations have resulted in the creation of a larger structure. One example of this is the well known economic success of Hong Kong, a tiny island and the only place in the world that has grown at mobilization rates for any significant length of time. Hong Kong's success was the result of the self-organizing systems with no intervention from the government. Hong Kong's living standard has already surpassed that of Britain, Canada, France and Australia. Another example is the Internet. There is no leader controlling it and yet it has developed in very fast and complex ways. In a way, every computer is the whole Internet, because every computer can access any piece of information on the Internet. The Internet owed its existence to the confluence of four main forces: the ongoing evolution of interconnected networks; the presence of large numbers of personal computers on local area networks that could be connected to the bigger network via a "universal gauge;" the spread of multimedia to personal computers; and the Berners-Lee's search method which is the method of hyper-linking key words on web pages.

Many people believe that had Darwinian innovation and self-organizing systems been allowed over the last twenty years in the US medical system, medical costs would easily be one-third lower today and health care access nearly universal. Because until quite recently, health care organization was anything but Darwinian. Today, with 95% of hospital charges and 80% of doctors' fees paid by insurers or governments, few Americans care what prices they have to pay for medical services. The result is an astonishingly oversized and bureaucratic health care industry where paper alone accounts for more than 25% of the nation's health care bill.

In its emphasis on the stress that necessarily accompanies evolutionary development, the "Red Queen Principle" is related to the generalized "Peter Principle". The Peter Principle, first introduced by L. Peter in a humoristic book describing the pitfalls of bureaucratic organization, states that in a hierarchically structured administration, people tend to be promoted up to their "level of incompetence." The principle is based on the observation that in such an organization new employees typically start in the lower ranks, but when they prove to be competent in the task to which they are assigned, they get promoted to a higher rank. This process of climbing up the hierarchical ladder can go on indefinitely, until the employee reaches a position where he or she is no longer competent. At that moment the process typically stops, since the established rules of bureaucracies make that it is very difficult to "demote" someone to a lower rank, even if that person would be much better fitted and more happy in that lower position. The net result is that most of the higher levels of a bureaucracy will be eventually filled by incompetent people, who got there because they were quite good at doing a different, and most often simpler and easier task than the one they are expected to do.

The evolutionary generalization of the principle is less pessimistic in its implications, since evolution lacks the bureaucratic inertia that pushes and maintains people in an unfit position. But what will certainly remain is that systems confronted by evolutionary problems will quickly tackle the easy ones, but tend to get stuck in the difficult ones. The better (more fit, smarter, more competent, more adaptive) a system is, the more quickly it will solve all the easy problems, but the more difficult the problem it finally gets stuck in will be. Getting stuck here does not mean "being unfit," it just means having reached the limit of one's competence, and thus having great difficulty advancing further. This explains why even the most complex and adaptive species (such as ourselves, humans) are still "struggling for survival" in their niches as energetically as the most primitive organisms such as bacteria. If ever a species would get control over all its evolutionary problems, then the "Red Queen Principle" would make sure that new, more complex problems would arise, so that the species would continue to balance on the border of its domain of incompetence. In conclusion, the generalized "Peter Principle" states that in evolution systems tend to develop up to the limit of their adaptive competence.

In a complex adaptive system, an agent that is resistant to change and not adaptable will have low fitness level. Conversely, an agent that is oversensitive to shifts in the external environment and continuously making radical responses will also have low fitness. In between the two extremes of stasis and chaos lies a region where fitness can be maximized - the edge the chaos. At that point one is simultaneously conservative and radical. Evolution is adept at keeping things at work while at the same time making very bold experiments. Nature has experimented wildly with this idea, resulting in vertebrates that range from birds to whales to humans.

At the **edge of chaos** one is simultaneously conservative and radical. Evolution is adept at keeping things a work while at the same time making bold experiments.

Kauffman imbued the edge if chaos with biological reality when he proposed the notion of the fitness landscape. To visualize a fitness landscape, picture a physical landscape with a series of peaks and valleys of varying heights and depths. In its struggle for survival, each species will attempt to move to higher and higher points, and in doing so it changes the landscape for other species with which it is co-evolving.

Kauffman uses the example of a fly and a frog. Both have their fitness landscapes but they are not independent. The frog shoots out its tongue and zap the fly is gone. Now imagine the fly evolves slippery feet so that the frog's tongue no longer stick anymore. The frog goes without dinner and its peak on the fitness landscape goes down, it is now less fit. The fly is fitter and so its peak rises. The whole landscapes changed as a result. Then the next stage is the that frog's tongue evolves into something that is able to catch the fly again.

Fitness changes, landscape changes - predator and prey constantly trying to be one step ahead of each other.

Kauffman observes that in the competition for survival, species attempt to alter their genetic make-up by taking "adaptive walks" to move to higher "fitness points", where their viability will be enhanced. Species who fail to move to higher points on their landscapes may be outpaced by competitors who are more successful in doing so, and risk becoming extinct through a process of natural selection.

But in nature, there seems to be limits on the speed with which species can climb peaks on their fitness landscapes. Darwin saw the process of evolution occurring at a gradual pace, with species gradually accumulating useful variations over extended periods of time through the process of natural selection. If a species is unable to evolve gradually, i.e. if the pace of change exceeds the capacity of the species to adapt and mutate by reassembling its building blocks, it will face extinction. The trigger for such rapid change could take the form of an "Error Catastrophe," which occurs when the rate of errors or miscopying of genetic code exceeds a critical " Error Threshold," and information within a species is completely lost (Eigen and Oswatitsch, 1992). Error catastrophe can lead a species to move down a peak if it occurs more quickly than the species can climb through natural selection processes. Useful traits acquired through natural selection can thus be lost, and the species drifts down its peak towards a valley on its fitness landscape.

Drawing the concept of co-evolution into a species' climb up peaks on its fitness landscape, Kauffman describes a co-evolutionary struggle between "Predator" and "Prey" species, in which the former develops a slightly better predation method that is subsequently countered by a new protection innovation by the latter, and so on. An example of a co-evolutionary struggle is the on-going battle between police and organized criminals to develop better new and innovative technologies to improve their ability to prevent and commit crimes respectively. The game goes on between drug enforcement officers and drugs smugglers as each tries to outsmart the other. As each group develops a new innovation, it alters the fitness landscape of the other - making a comfortable local peak appear to shrink. Door locks dating from the 1960s are swift work for thieves of today and ever improving and innovative security devices for credit cards from hologram to microchips are coming into use to prevent credit card fraud.

The fitness of any particular location on the fitness landscape is not an objective and identical value for every species. In a fixed environment, certain higher fitness points will have more value to some species than to others. Geneticists describe the process of "epistatic coupling", in which a new gene links into the network of a species' existing genes. These coupling interactions between new and existing genes mean the contribution a new gene can make to a species' overall fitness depends on genes the species already has. For example, a long neck would be more useful to a giraffe, which already has long legs and can use such a neck to reach treetop leaves, than to a hippopotamus, whose short legs are designed to allow it to eat grass. And as species become more complicated, the network of existing genes with which a new gene must epistatically couple grows, increasing the probability of internal conflict within the species over the value of a particular step in its adaptive walk on the fitness landscape. It becomes more and more difficult for a species to evaluate whether a new gene will improve its overall fitness, reducing the chance that such an improvement will take place. A high density of epistatic connections thus slows the speed with which the species can consider new variations and evolve. Because the fitness landscape surrounding a species depends to a great extent on the characteristics of that species itself, the landscape surrounding a species with a high number of epistatic connections will have more hills and valleys, containing many lower "compromise" peaks rather than one easily apparent optimal peak.

Kauffman began to apply this concept of fitness landscapes to the evolution of technology in organizations. He asserts that firms embark on adaptive walks to develop new technologies, traveling up peaks on their landscapes. Each movement up a local peak reduces the number of directions in which the technology can be improved by a constant fraction, so climbing becomes more difficult. This claim appears to be supported by evidence that as technologies mature, each additional dollar invested yields a steadily declining marginal improvement. The increasing number of epistatic connections means that what may be a desirable improvement for one part of the technological innovation may negatively affect another part. If a firm or individual happens to be in a fitness valley, then mutation and selection might push it up a local peak, meaning a rise in fitness. Once on a local peak it may, metaphorically, gaze enviously at a nearby peak, but be unable to reach it because that would require crossing valleys of lower fitness.

Chapter 8
back to
S|trategy|

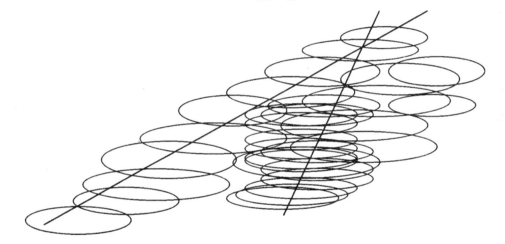

Back to Strategy

Several management researchers have drawn powerful analogies between organizations and complex adaptive systems with the notion of adaptive agents evolving and changing their internal models as a result of exploitation and exploration behavior, against a background of non-linear interactions. This rings true for players in organizational life.

Vriend (1994) described a "complex system" as one consisting of "a large number of agents that interact with each other in various ways," and such a system as "adaptive" if these agents change their actions as a result of the events in the process of interaction. A collection of firms each striving to achieve a competitive advantage over one another, and adjusting their strategies accordingly, clearly meets with Vriend's definition. Profit outcomes are jointly determined by the interactions of the firms (and their strategies), while the ability of firms to alter their actions over time is evidence of adaptive behavior. Even a struggle of political coalitions within a firm to determine strategic agendas can be viewed as a complex adaptive system.

In a business setting, a complex adaptive system (a business or multi-business firm) is composed of interacting "agents" (employees, managers, board members, suppliers, alliances, regulators etc.) following rules (blue prints, values, ethics, law, economics, industry structures, value appropriation) exchanging influence (ideas, products, technology, know-how, contracts, money) with their local and global environments (from the cubicle to the global market) and altering the very environment they are responding by virtue of their "simple" actions. Complex adaptive systems of all kinds, from ecosystem to multinational corporations, share dozens of fundamental characteristics and processes - from to co-evolution to punctuated equilibrium to path dependence - that make the study of one so pertinent to the understanding of the other.

In competitive situations in the biological world, predators and prey must continuously co-evolve by adjusting to the adaptation of their opponents. It is possible for groups of species to reach a local optimum in a fitness landscape (much like an extended transient in the Game of Life may survive for an indefinite number of periods) but each species must be able to adapt very rapidly if the environment changes in such a way as to make their behavior sub-optimal. Thus a change in the environment may cause an "arms race" or evolutionary spurt until a local optimum is again being reached.

Sounds something like industries best practices? Much evidence suggest that industries are like a "red queen" race. Studies of the performance of firms in the long run reveal that many firms have difficulty maintaining superior performance for any extended period of time, and generally few can do it more than five years. Companies that succeed in escaping velocity do so through continuous innovation and adaptation which enables them to become the fastest runner in the "red queen" race. In a competitive business environment, relative progress ("running") is necessary just for maintenance ("staying put"), meaning that all Business Process Re-engineering or Total Quality Management in the world will only able to help businesses to stay where they are, not to move forward. When Merck acquired Medco, a mail-order provider of drug and health benefits, the acquisition completely changed the landscape of the pharmaceutical industry. But within months, all of Merck's top competitors had responded with acquisitions of their own.

> In this **competitive** world, relative progress ("running") is necessary just for maintenance ("staying put"), meaning that all BPR or TQM will only able to help businesses to stay put, but not to move forward.

In the biological world, "punctuated Equilibrium" makes it difficult for members to survive for long periods of time, as their strategies and skills are usually optimized for the rather stable periods and then suddenly become obsolete when the inevitable restructuring takes place. Similarly, companies have a hard time surviving the upheavals, shakeouts and technology discontinuities that punctuate the markets. Looking back, it was not Sears that created the category killer stores or the once booming mail-order industry, despite the fact that Sears had actually invented the catalog almost five previously ago; rather it was strategic innovators such as Wal-Mart, Home Depot and Lands' End. IBM is another example. It was not the industry giant and father of computing, who pioneered the personal computer, the desktop computer or the work station, or even the Internet and groupware like Notes; rather new entrants like Sun, Apple, Silicone Graphics, Lotus and Netscape. Though both IBM and Sears did survive the storm, they have been less dynamic in their industries and have suffered an extended period of financial under-performance

In the emerging study of complex systems, the constraints of a system's history on its current behavior, which has been labeled as "path dependence," is manifested in a wide range of systems. In biological systems, the evolution of a species may depend on random events in the life of a founder, or on stochastic processes that affect the interactions between species or exert selection pressures. Organizations may also be shaped by path-dependent processes and events.

Applying the concept of cellular automata to the business environment, many chaos theorists have linked the present business world to Class III system, i.e. a randomly chaotic system with no predictability. It appears to me, however, that there is plenty of evidence to support the view that the business world is a complex system poised on the "edge of chaos," - a Class IV system - rather than a system in a state of perpetual chaos.

There are a host of factors causing environmental turbulence today: the globalization of markets; economic deregulation; the computing and digital communication revolution; breakthroughs in biotechnology and genetic engineering; and the increasing importance of global environmental and security issues. However, it is important to note that not all industries are affected equally by these changes, and that different firms will experience them at different times. The degree of turbulence more likely follows a power-law distribution with some periods in history having a much higher level of turbulence than others. Many industries appear to go through long periods of incremental change with the occasional discontinuous change or punctuated equilibrium. Indeed much research on technological discontinuities has revealed a whole typology of change ranging from minor process improvements to completely new product-market classes. Smaller improvements would seem to be much more numerous than large-scale improvements.

A further characteristics of Class IV systems is that they might even experience a sharp increase in turbulence during rare periods. The system might even become chaotic for a short period of time before being pulled back to the edge of chaos. The 1950s and 1960s appeared to be relatively calm periods of economic growth, so it is clear that the business system is also capable of becoming less turbulent and more like a Class II system.

And on a more anecdotal level, leaders in a wide range of industries tend to hold their positions for relatively long periods of time (often for decades), suggesting that their source of competitive advantage may be somewhat sustainable, or at least renewable, but not without effort. Examples of companies that have held a dominant position in their industry for many years include IBM, 3M, Ford, Kodak, Citibank, Coca-Cola, Shell, Johnson and Johnson, Exxon, AT&T, McDonalds and ICI. This is hardly the picture of unrestrained turbulence and unpredictability that many chaos theorists have claimed exists in today's business world.

What, then, are the implications for strategic planning?

A Class I system is a trivial case as the behavior tends to 'death' or zero. The next chart could well be classified as a Class I system.

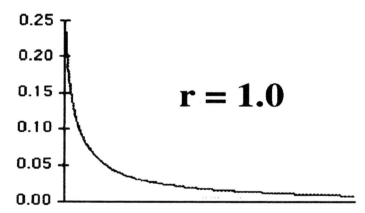

Output logistic equation for $r=1.0$

$r = 1.0$

In Class II system the behavior of the system is both stable and predictable. The stable and continuous economic growth of the 1950s and 1960s could be viewed as approximating a Class II system. Strategic planning is also a relatively trivial exercise in Class II systems. Planning is based on identifying repetitive although historical patterns and projecting them into the future (although such planning may of course be complicated by the presence of measurement error or complex business cycles that may revolve around eight or more points.)

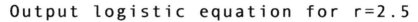

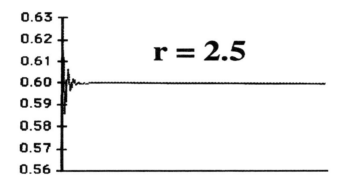

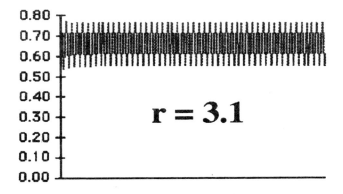

Class III or chaotic systems display a sensitivity dependence on initial conditions that makes accurate predictions of future conditions virtually impossible. Strategic planning is not possible in Class III systems beyond specifying the broad limits of the behavior of interest (e.g. snow is unlikely to fall in Boston in the summer, small companies are less likely to takeover large companies).

Class IV systems are an extremely interesting case. To the extent that extended transients in Class IV systems display regular (i.e. predictable) behavior for prolonged periods of time then it would seem that strategic planning is indeed possible. However, planners in a Class IV world should attempt a Stoic outlook on life. Although it can be assumed that extended transients will follow a fixed trajectory, it should be recognized that at any time an unforeseen interaction with a chaotic element or other transient in the system has the potential to divert or destroy the elements of the extended transient. In these situations, organizations should abandon strategic planning in favor of organizational learning and complex systems theory where the firm must learn to rapidly adapt to its ever-changing environment.

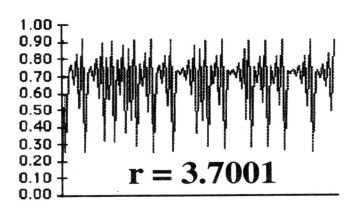

Output logistic equation for r=3.7001

r = 3.7001

But so-called strategic planning must also be recognized for what it is: a means, not to create strategy, but just to program a strategy which is already being created and to implement it formally. Strategic planning is essentially analytic in nature and built on decomposition, while strategy creation is essentially a process of synthesis. That is the reason why trying to create strategies through formal planning often leads to extrapolating existing strategies or copying those of competitors.

Trying to create strategies through formal planning processes often leads to extrapolating existing strategies or **copying** those of competitors.

Let us now bring the discussion to the level of a particular organization or industry. We have said that many of our strategies are systematically failing us because we have been choosing tools based on invalid assumptions. We have said that most businesses today move on the continuum of Class IV behavior. How is a manager to diagnose whether his business is a class II, III or IV system, so that he can respond with the appropriate strategy tools? Fundamental to this diagnosis is an understanding of the notion of uncertainty.

Uncertainty is a word that we often use but know very little about. Let us have a little science lesson here. In the late 1920s Werner Heisenberg shocked the academic world with his uncertainty principle of quantum mechanics. He showed that you can get closer and yet see less. Then he showed that the atoms in our brains are uncertain. Even with total information we still could not say things with 100% certainty. He demonstrated that even in physics the truth of statement is a matter of degree. He made the world face multi-valued logic, statements true or false or interminate to some degree.

Aristotle and other scientists and mathematicians had all believed that every "well-formed" statement was either true and false. Heisenberg made people question the bivalent logic that we have taken for granted for centuries just as Aristotle had taken it for granted. He made doubt scientific.

At that time probability theory was the only known way to put this doubt in math form. So rather than shifting us from black and white to gray truth, the uncertainty principle had the effect of shifting to the probability of all-or-none bivalent truth. There are some little-known facts about Heisenberg's uncertainty principle. Most people know quantum mechanics is strange and they know that Einstein's relativity bends light, slows clocks and measures the energy of nuclear explosions. And they know quantum mechanics is strange because light comes in quantal packets and behaves both as waves and particle. The truth is strange: If you drive very fast down a freeway in a straight line and watch your speedometer, then you may not know where your car sits in the freeway at that moment. If you drive fast enough, I mean faster than the other cars, then you cannot know how fast you drive. Speed or position - you pick one. The more you try to pin down your speed, the less you can pin down your position and vice versa. Here the speedometer actually disturbs nothing and merely measures the effects of the cause. The cause lies in the very nature of things. It is the linear math we attribute to things.

Even today, many scientists still believe that uncertainty relations were unique to quantum mechanics, but its relations arose from a math quirk. Nowadays we have built uncertainty relations into the structure of the information age. And natural selection seems to have built them into our brains.

Now back to the real of world of business and economics, ask yourself the following question:

> **Most strategic planning tools being used today are more like speedometers. Have we really been spending too much time looking at our speedometers?**

The best way to answer this question depends on where you are driving. If you are driving in the English countryside, it's good to look at your speedometer and check your speed limit. If you are driving on the interstate freeway, you kind of do both. But if you are on the racetrack, you only look at the cars around you. In many of today's industries, you are more likely to be driving on the race track.

Another way to put it is every system has a time horizon within which it behaves. Using the weather as an example, today we have thousands of weather stations and satellites up there to help us make weather forecasts. But none of them has changed the time horizon of weather forecasting, which is no more than a day at best. And only within this horizon can weather forecasts be precise enough. Some other systems have even shorter horizons. In ice hockey, there are a number of players and a set of rules. Over a few seconds or so, it is possible to predict what will happen. Someone starts hitting the ball, a good player can estimate where it will land and try to be there at that moment. But if we attempt to analyze the game – the position of each player, the speed and direction and the kind of pitch, we would never able be able to predict that a few minutes later a goal will be scored.

In business many companies try to do it and pay a lot of money for these predictions. Yet the real time horizon of business, depending on what industry one is in, may be only about two months. So determining the level of uncertainty of that industry is the first primary task.

Uncertainty can be broadly seen as having three levels:

Level one is characterized by a low level of uncertainty. At level one, traditional microeconomics frameworks are sufficient. One can more or less develop a snap-shot of the industry and reasonably predict the immediate future. There is a certain level of uncertainty but the analysis will be able to provide a scenario where a clear strategic direction can emerge. Industries with this level of uncertainty include mass merchandise, fast-foods, radio broadcasting, consumer durables, luxury goods, and automobiles, where change over the last ten years has been evolutionary, allowing many companies to base their strategy on a prediction.

At level two, analysis will show that the future will follow one of a few discrete scenarios, though it will be pretty difficult to predict which one. Outcomes in different scenarios are in many cases heavily influenced by government regulations, political forces and dramatic moves by industry key players or new entrants. Scenario planning, quantitative game theory and options pricing frameworks will be necessary to determine a strategy with options. Since the number of scenarios will be limited to four or less, strategy can be determined analytically. Industries with this level of uncertainty include telecoms; media broadcasting or publishing; fashionable goods; chemicals and other commodities; and natural resources industries such as mining, energy and exploration.

At level three there are multiple and complex dimensions of continuous uncertainty. The most obvious of industries that fall into this category are biotech, drugs discoveries, communications technologies, Internet technologies and computer industries. There are high levels of uncertainty over consumer adoption and demand. Disruption results from the effects of any move by strategic partners or suppliers and technological discontinuities or breakthroughs. A planning cycle in these industries is often less than one year. Take the

PC hardware business for example, now you are talking about 10 to 14 months per cycle, and in software no more than 6 months. For a new Internet site, three months is probably the most. At level three, only the complexity theory approach to strategy seems to make sense. Here managers must learn to recognize the dynamics inherent in every situation and manage the building blocks of strategy effectively over time through a guided evolutionary process. One good example is Chiron Corp., considered by many in the financial markets to be a biotech blue chip. The nineteen-year-old company has been expanding dramatically since Ciba Geigy purchased a 49.9 % stake, and now has over 6,000 staff. Chiron discovered a vaccine for Hepatitis C virus, and was first to sequence the HIV genome and use this information to make recombinant versions of HIV proteins. Chiron's strategy is to try to manage chaos. This is appropriate for a company such as Chiron because opportunities in biotechnology don't come in any predictable fashion. When opportunities come, the company must immediately reassess its priorities so they must have a management system that allows frequent disruptions of plans.

Levels of Uncertainty

HIGH LEVEL OF UNCERTAINTY

Complex Adaptive Systems
Learning Organization
Evolutionary Strategy
Increasing Return

Leverage of Core-Competencies
Core-Competencies Building
Game theory
Scenario Planning

Microeconomic Models
Five-Forces Analysis
Industry / Product Lifecycles
Experience Curves

LOW LEVEL OF UNCERTAINTY

Any strategy requires a choice about posture. A strategic posture defines the strategic intent relative to the current and future state of the industry, and strategic postures have been categorized into three kinds:

First there are "shapers," whose aim is to drive their industries toward a new structure and whose mission is to re-invent the game. Through strategic innovation and challenging the rules of the game they create new opportunities and value either by shaking up a relatively stable industry or by pushing the market into a new direction. To be successful, a strategic innovation has to be "ripped" - there has to be receptivity to the concept. All other postures exploit a change that has already happened or at least is beginning to occur. They satisfy a need that already exists. But "shapers" bring about the change. They aims at creating a want. No one can tell in advance whether the user is going to be receptive, indifferent or actively resistant. In most cases, receptivity is a big gamble. And the odds are unknown.

The second posture is the "strategic adapter." The strategic adapter takes the current industry structure and its future evolution as givens, and reacts to the opportunities the market offers by using tools such as value-chain analysis and five-forces analysis. They pick a clear strategic position on where and how to compete in the current market under existing or readily predictable conditions.

The third posture is "options writers" who come in two forms. The first is typically large companies with deep pockets and access to relatively cheap cost of capital, who can afford to place multiple bets and wait until the dust settles. They then move forward with full scale large capital commitment and achieve large economies of scales. The second form usually consists of small Silicon Valley types of start-up that have multiple projects moving at the same time and change strategic direction any time the competitive landscape or the environment changes. Strategy comes only after the environment becomes less uncertain, if it does. In many cases, the direction set by the senior management would be combined with short communication lines and channels to their managers and workers in real-time, rather than a periodic review and adjustment of the strategy. Large corporations in high technology industries tend to prefer options writer postures. They will face less risk and uncertainty as they will only exploit a change which is both likely and imminent. Very often their investments are huge and irreversible, such as a new semi-conductor fabrications plant for a new kind of chip.

The three strategic postures

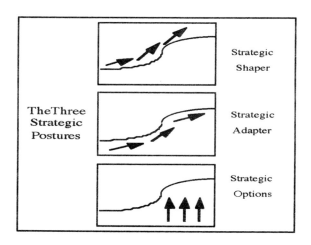

Very often the reasons behind how companies choose their strategic postures and strategy tools lie in their dominant logic which, as we have seen, can be very hard to shift. In complex adaptive systems, companies may need to change their strategic postures as the outcome of their own and others' strategies changes the competitive landscape.

At the heart of this lies a complex challenge in becoming an evolver as well as a competitor. To prosper in the long run, a company must as good at managing its strategic evolution as it is at managing its market. It must be both a tough competitor and a flexible and smart evolver, and be able to change its strategic postures depending on the situation. This means excelling at conflicting goals simultaneously: you need strategies that are both focused robust; strategies that enable you to adapt continuously; operating conservatively and innovating radically; maintaining diversity yet establishing standards and routines; optimizing scale and maintaining flexibility. Historically, the equilibrium view of strategy has focused on achieving a sustainable competitive advantage, but not on "strategic flexibility," and strategy tools based on equilibrium help us to be good competitors, but not evolvers. There are obvious tensions and contradictions between the two and it's not that one can just strike a middle ground. Managers need to be able to manage and guide the strategic evolution process. The name of the game is "guided evolution" not securing or sustaining competitive advantage.

The growth of a large business is merely a survival of the **fittest**.

As new ideas and strategy concepts based on complexity theory are being developed, we will be seeing new tools such as modeling using option theory. New organization forms will be invented to help avert complexity catastrophe. Becoming a good evolver will become an enormous challenge for companies. It will be difficult to convince a successful company that is enjoying good economic rent to take on the task of becoming more innovative and adaptive to meet new challenges that it can never foresee. Equally, a company struggling for survival will argue that it makes no sense to worry about the its long-term evolvability when it is not sure of its short-term survivability. For those companies and leaders that chose to accept the challenges, the payoff promises to be big. Through the science of complexity, we can come to understand how evolution works and the skills and organization forms that are needed to survive or prosper in a complex world.

Chapter 9

the competencies and knowledge landscape

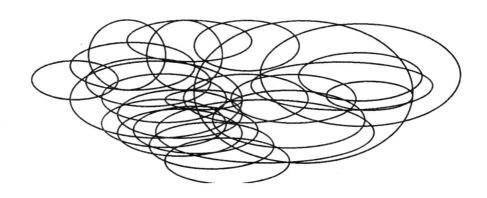

The competencies and knowledge landscape

I propose that the fitness landscape of an organization competing in today's knowledge economy consists of the knowledge and competencies that the organization possesses or is able to build and leverage. Recall for a moment the series of peaks and valleys of varying height, depth, and steepness on a species' fitness landscape. Now shift the unit of analysis from that of a species to that of a company operating in the knowledge economy, for example a software or drugs development company. The key success factor for such a firm is the competencies and knowledge it develops and leverages. This means that in its struggle for survival, a company will attempt to move to higher and higher points on a competencies and knowledge landscape. That is, instead of "fitness," the peaks on the organization's landscape represent knowledge and competencies, or in some cases potential knowledge and competencies; maybe we do not consider competencies or knowledge to exist in a more tangible form "out there," but as something that can only be developed within an individual, then shared through interaction and interpretation in an organizational entity.

I have no doubt that we have already passed the entrance portal of the knowledge era. Its advent is coming to expression in a variety of ways. The advance of human knowledge in the last few decades of this century has outstripped all the combined discoveries and advances of human knowledge throughout history. Production based mainly on knowledge and information is becoming the major source of human wealth - just look at the wealth created by the technology start-ups for the last five years. The development and advance of new directions of production such as biotech or new materials depends foremost on their knowledge base. The knowledge element becomes the crucial factor in the advance and success of agriculture, services, and industry. Knowledge workers become an increasingly important, essential element of the workforce and are in heavy demand globally. With the rise in the centrality of knowledge and information comes the growing importance of the media and others who handle and direct the flow of information. The thread tying all the major changes in modes of human production and wealth creation together is the quantum leap in the importance of the knowledge component.

Today the success of an enterprise depends increasingly on the quality of its people in terms of the level of knowledge, information, and know-how at their disposal. Countries or societies with a greater ability to acquire knowledge and information more quickly can easily become rich. Knowledge is substituting savings and replacing other resources such as energy, materials, warehouse facilities and transportation. Knowledge is also becoming the key factor in global power struggles, replacing power conflicts over material and energy resources.

Before we move on, let me briefly define "knowledge" and "competencies." Using a resource based view, a firm is seen as a portfolio of resources rather than a portfolio of products or product-markets. The term "resources" can refer to competencies and knowledge. Knowledge can be classified into three types: information, know-how and insights. Information refers to data and facts, things that can be stored and exchanged easily, it tells us what something is all about. Know-how refers to the accumulated knowledge of how to do something in a different or more effective way. This might include skills, routines, operating procedures, organization forms and even relationships with other parties. Insights denote the comprehension of a theory or model of the underlying mechanism for observed causal relationships. It is a generalization that comes from experience of many instances of cause-effect relationships and mental logic or mental models. Competencies, have been defined in many different ways. Hamel and Prahalad (1994) define competencies as the current skills of the firm and the accumulation of intellectual capital. Leonard-Barton (1992) uses a slightly different term, "Core Capability", which is the knowledge sets including skills, technical systems, managerial systems and values that distinguishes one firm from another. The differences are really very minor.

Competencies and knowledge landscapes share several similarities with fitness landscapes:

Adaptive Walks - Species on fitness landscapes take "adaptive walks," climbing peaks in order to improve their chances of survival. Organizations on competencies and knowledge landscapes take "Knowledge Development Expeditions", intentionally exploring for and developing new, potential knowledge and competencies.

The Dynamic of Fitness Improvement - Organizations, like species, are concerned with simultaneous survival and advancement, and "move" to improve their fitness on their own competencies and knowledge landscapes. I suggest that the "dynamics" of the competencies and knowledge landscape resemble those of its fitness counterpart, and in moving on their competencies and knowledge landscapes, companies that succeed in the long term engage in two simultaneous activities: survival and advancement, meaning climbing and exploring. These activities occur simultaneously and on all scales in the organization, that is, across hierarchical level, geographical location, and over time, often happening at the same time, with any one activity interrelated to the other.

Climbing Local Peaks - Climbing is a "survival" activity, in which the firm moves up a potential competencies and knowledge peak that consists of data sources of which the firm is aware. A firm is simultaneously open and closed on different scales. The open part allows the firm to take in and structurally couple with the data sources that make up the peak, such as knowledgeable individuals and centers of excellence in a particular technology. The closed part of a firm is the place where data is discussed and self-referenced to create knowledge, as well as where epistatic coupling occurs. We recall from Kauffman's model that the more extensive the interconnectedness of a species or firm, the more difficult it will be for data "signals" to lead to knowledge development and changes in the firm's internal rules, therefore the steeper the local peak becomes for the firm.

Exploring the Landscape -The firm may also engage in exploratory "advancement" activities to identify new competencies and knowledge peaks of which it is as yet unaware. Sub-units of the organization can fan out to explore broader regions of the landscape, evaluate the height and steepness of nearby peaks to move up non-local peaks. Exploration activities can lead to the appearance of entirely new peaks on the competencies and knowledge landscape, as the firm unintentionally deforms its landscape every time it climbs or explores. The firm can even intentionally deform the landscape to improve its position, and undertake actions that will lead the local peak to rise, or others to decline. For example, a firm can "hop" or intentionally cause a chain reaction to deform its landscape and make its own peak rise, by publicly announcing new products, markets or a change in strategic direction. Exploration is a means of realizing Schumperterian innovation by combining existing resources in a unique novel way. It leads to both value creation as the exploration activities cause new peaks to appear on the landscape, and value appropriation as the firm's intentional or unintentional deformation of the landscape causes other peaks to be lowered.

Contrasting Activities
Between Survival and Advancement

(Survival)	**(Advancement)**
Climbing Local Peak	**Exploring Local Peaks**
Re-Engineering	Re-Invention
Negative Feedback	Positive Feedback
Internal Restructuring	External Alliances
Following Rules	Inventing Rules
Hierarchy	Network
Optimization	Experimentation

Advancement Activities

Continuous to explore new opportunities, develop new competencies and challenge industry rules while constantly look for external strategic alliances.

Edge of Chaos - Between the two extremes of stasis and chaos lies the region where fitness is maximized. Here one is simultaneously conservative and radical.

Survival Activities

Manage facilities for volume growth, repetitive operational tasks and maximum efficiencies in a deeply conservative and tightly controlled fashion.

Co-evolution

Shifts on the landscape may also be caused by interactions with other organizations. The firm is not alone on its local peaks, nor on its competencies and knowledge landscape as a whole. Other individuals, units, or firms may see the same potential knowledge peaks, even though each peak will have a different shape depending on who is looking and from where. Every step any firm takes in its survival or advancement efforts, causes reverberations felt by everyone else operating on that competencies and knowledge landscape. The reverberations caused by these interactions are highly sensitive to increasing returns to scale and positive feedback, and can ultimately lead to avalanches of change, possibly governed by the principle of self-organized criticality.

Microsoft's relatively late entry into the Internet browser industry has shifted the landscape for competitors such as Netscape, who now face many much steeper peaks. Amazon.com's entry into book retailing shifted the landscape and resulted in established players such as Borders or Barnes and Noble facing steeper peaks. Barnes and Noble's later decision to enter into Internet book retailing further shifted the landscape and reduced the fitness of Amazon.com. In turn Amazon.com's entry into Internet music retailing shaped the landscape for people such as HMV or Tower Records. Amazon.com's acquisition of Drugstore.com changed the dynamics of drugs retailing.

The Internet has already turned the publishing, insurance, banking and travel industries upside down and it will do the same to every industry.

Co-evolutionary reverberations are almost impossible to predict. When Bell Atlantic and cable giant Tele-Communications Inc. announced plans to merge in 1994, their stated intention was to build a nation-wide network to deliver interactive "content" to homes across the US. But the announcement led to a wave of articles and discussion about the coming information superhighway, shifting the competencies and knowledge landscape for all firms touching this industry. Some competencies and knowledge peaks were perceived to grow, leading many firms to make strategic choices to announce large infrastructure spending programs. The wave of investment meant the merged company would face more competition than it had anticipated, and also meant Bell Atlantic could ride on other people's transmission network instead of owning one with TCI. The resulting changes on Bell Atlantic's landscape led it to pursue other options, and the merger was abandoned after only four months had passed.

Firms that are climbing the same local competencies and knowledge peak may end up in a co-evolutionary struggle. A current example of this would be Netscape and Microsoft, who are both racing to develop knowledge about a market that is still forming: Internet service provision. Particularly in the knowledge economy, these races among two or more firms to reach the top of one particular peak can lead to faster and faster rates of competencies and knowledge development, and taken to the extreme, may lead to co-evolutionary "arms races." In these situations, the firms have to work harder and harder to develop knowledge and climb the peak faster than their competitors in a "Red Queen" effect. In such a scenario, the firm constantly changes its survival strategy, eventually reaching a point at which it is unable to reassemble its useable building blocks sufficiently quickly to keep moving up its peak.

In addition to the above characteristics largely shared between fitness and competencies and knowledge landscapes, I suggest that competencies and knowledge landscapes include another important characteristic which has not yet been associated with fitness landscapes. Competencies and knowledge landscapes seem to be inherently fractal, with self-similar patterns observable on different levels of scale. The concept of scale relates to the multi-level, hierarchical design of nature, where objects have the same shape regardless of size. Scale is what allows us to conceive of the complex adaptive systems notion of fractals. In much the same way that each fractal part of an object contains elements of the whole, each peak on the competencies and knowledge landscape consists of an entire landscape of its own. Similarly, on a higher level of scale, a firm's competencies and knowledge landscape can be viewed as a single peak on the competencies and knowledge landscape facing a group of firms, or an industry. The notion of scale means that instead of being completely in one place on one competencies and knowledge landscape, the firm is in fact simultaneously in several places, on several competencies and knowledge landscapes

Consider Cisco, the $120 billion 15 year old start-up which is the now the fifteenth largest in the world. Their routers have enabled companies, government and universities to link their computing resources into large-scale networks of shared information and real-time communications. Having established unquestioned leadership in the enterprise data networking market, Cisco is now setting its sights on competing with Lucent, Nortel and Ericsson in the areas of providing network infrastructure for telecommunications providers. Cisco is attempting to advance in a new fitness landscape caused by the accelerating convergence of voice and data communications. Despite its huge success and knowledge of data communications, Cisco has to climb a new fitness landscape and take "knowledge development expeditions," and it is no longer a 800 pound gorilla since it will be competing with competitors with resources equal if not larger than its own. The real challenge for Cisco is to build networks that are reliable, robust and scalable as their current voice networks, and this is something it has never done before. And doing so will lead to reverberations deforming the entire knowledge landscape for all other organizations operating in the same time-space continuum such as Lucent, Nortel and Ericsson.

Most companies don't die because they are wrong; they die because they do not commit themselves. The greatest **danger** is standing still.

By suggesting the concept of the competencies and knowledge landscape, I have challenged the existing assumptions in the literature concerning the operation of firms in their own environments - the source theory coming from complex adaptive systems and in particular its concept of the fitness landscape. Backed by this new perspective of the competencies and knowledge landscape, what view of the organization emerges? How can this assist managers to better understand the kind of organization that does continuously adapt? In other words, how does a firm successfully operate on this landscape? An organization which is caught between simultaneous survival and advancement activities on different scales in time and space, achieves success by continuous climbing and exploring to exploit the dynamics of its landscape, interacts and co-evolves with other firms, and considers lower-scale issues within itself. The traditional approach to strategy is based on the notion of "fit", aligning the company's internal strength with the external environment. Complexity theory suggests that organizations respond best to fundamental change if they are not perfectly aligned with their environment but poised on the "edge of chaos." To be able to do this, there are key things a company must do:

KEY THINGS A COMPANY MUST DO :

- Avoid **over reliance** on an incumbent management team. In many cases the more senior the management the greater attachment they have to the existing dominant logic and close adherence to the status quo.

- Avoid **excessive 'fit'**. In order to challenge the status quo and be able to innovate, there needs to be enough organizational slack for the firm to develop strategic options alongside the main strategy.

- Allow **diversity** and try to rotate people regularly so that they can disseminate their own experience and gain further insights from people in other parts of the business. Use outsiders from different backgrounds, industries and cultures. Ensure that cultures and organizations do not ossify into homogeneous concrete, but remain sufficiently fluid for the organization to change and adapt.

- Don't avoid **mistakes**. The only way to gain and sustain a competitive advantage when there is no sustainable competitive advantage is to ensure that your organization knows what to learn and that it is learning faster than the competition. Making mistakes faster than the competitors gives you more chances to learn and win.

- Allow **experimentation** and encourage parallel developments. Try to learn from failure. Complexity theory emphasizes process and organizational dynamics at the expense of content and analysis. Experimentation is necessary in the strategy making process. Encourage parallel developments because in a world where the future is unknown, sticking too closely to the knitting can be dangerous.

- Foster the development of **new skills** such as listening, reflecting and questioning that enable employees to effectively perform and collaborate at the edge of chaos.

- Design **performance metrics** that distinguishes between legacy businesses and future growth options. Organizations should measure future growth options as a venture capitalist would.

- Design personnel **evaluation** processes and incentives systems that distinguish between good ideas that were well executed but unsuccessful and people who are unsuccessful.

- Avoid pursue relatively **singular strategies** and thus occupy only one spot on the landscape. Ask yourself how many strategies is each business simultaneously pursuing or are they just different initiatives pursuing the same strategy?

The Skills of Complex Adaptive Organization, as practiced by every member of the organization

CEO	Leader	Team Member	Individual
Radar Screen Monitoring	Facilitating Group Process	Applying Knowledge Competence	Questioning, Listening, Reflecting
Facilitating Strategic Dialogue	Collaborative Coaching	Contributing as a Team Member	Understanding
Action Modeling	Managing Change	Leading Teams	Leveraging Knowledge
Mental Modeling	Strategic Thinking	Running a Micro-Business	Learning to Learn

One example of a company that understands this is Monsanto, a once chemical conglomerate which is now transforming itself into a life-sciences powerhouse. The company is now entering a new phase in its transformation and for the last few years has been focusing on finding and climbing new peaks, and assembling the necessary capabilities to become the leader in life-sciences. They did this through building capabilities for a science-based nutrition platform and acquired three seed business, DEKALP Genetics Corp., Plant Breeding International Cambridge Ltd., and the international seed business of Cargill Inc. The have also reorganized themselves to foster opening, innovation and initiative, and most of all the ability to act quickly and decisively. For example they designed a "box buddies" system in which they teamed up two people and work located them in adjoining cubicles, keeping each other posted about what's happening with the latest events. Monsanto's three year old system known internally as "Two in a Box," pairs a scientist with a marketing or financial specialist in dozens of critical management positions. In the company's giant agricultural sector, for instance, thirty pairs of box buddies lead most of the crop and geographical teams. Monsanto is betting that this unusual structure will help its transformation. By joining its commercial and research departments at the head, the company is seeking a jump-start in developing breakthrough genetic technologies and bringing them to market faster than its competitors.

The password for success is "Let a hundred flowers bloom" rather than "bring in more clones" and managers should emphasize shifts from top-down command and control to **self-organization**.

Chapter 10

strategy

as a

guided

evolutionary

process

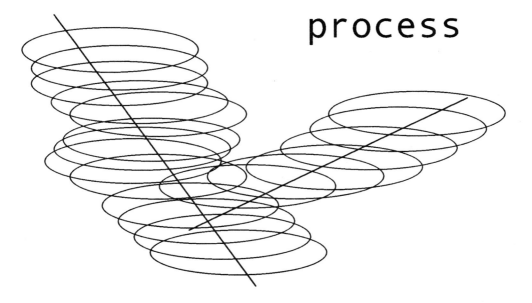

Strategy as a guided evolutionary process

Now let's perceive an organization as an ecological environment specifically designed to guide the growth of different species, which in this case are different products, services or technology innovations. These are different fitness landscapes within the organization. The management's role under this concept will be to help to create and guide evolutionary processes within this organization, which helps the firm to adapt to changes in the environment, which in turn leverages the evolutionary and ecological forces to manage the processes of formulating and implementing a strategy. These forces work within the existing systems of the organization and alter the original dynamics of the firm's strategy, ultimately affecting the performance of the firm.

Let's consider Sun Microsystems, a computer company once specialized in workstations running Unix for computer-aided design users and computer animators. With the Java buzz Sun has now grown to deafening proportions. The Internet craze provides one clue as to the reason for this growth, and the prevailing quest for any technology that threatens Microsoft provides the other. Java was designed by four programmers at Sun as an experimental project which never received much attention or support. One day these four programmers decided to leave Sun and sent out e-mails to everyone including all their bosses and the CEO, complaining about the firm's management. Scott McNealy, Sun's CEO, decided to see them the next day and seek out the problem. They showed him their smart Java applets - simple programs that can be delivered over the network - enlivened and animated Web pages at a time when users were bored with static web pages. These applets were loaded across the network and executed locally without access to the hard disk - and without exposing individual systems to serious security risks. They also promised cross-platform compatibility.

McNealy looked at the idea and realized that this could become hot technology overnight, bringing Sun into new competitive space. These applets raised Java's profile so high that even Microsoft, in late 1995, contacted Sun about licensing Java to use in its browser, Internet Explorer, just as Netscape had done months earlier for its own browser. Java's potential to trump Windows has further driven the hype. Competing companies are cooperating with Java because they see it as their last hope in the battle against Microsoft. The world has long wanted an open alternative platform to Microsoft.

Next consider Polaroid, the famous company that invented and created the instant photography industry and that has a powerful brand name internationally. It was founded by Edwain Land, a scientist who led the company through a decade of technological and marketing successes. In the early 1980s, Land believed the company needed to diversify in order to reduce the vulnerability of its core business. He took the company into numerous new ventures involving such products as disk drives, video recorders, ink jet printers, fiber optics and medical diagnostic equipment.

After two generations of CEO, Gary DiCamillo assumed leadership in 1995. He gave each division responsibility for setting strategy, developing products, and marketing products on a global basis, with corresponding accountability for sales, profits and management of assets. And because digital imaging technologies met the needs of the markets delineated for all three areas, development of digital technologies was widely dispersed throughout the company. He discovered that the staff he inherited possessed a high level of technical competency geared to the core business of instant photography, i.e. many were chemical engineers whose skills were of little use to the digital arena. He therefore instituted an effort to attract talented professionals away from other digital and high technology companies, and did not rule out the possibility of further supplements and replacements in Polaroid's future to keep pace with fundamental changes in technology occurring in different parts of the business.

The first product to emerge from all these efforts was a 1991 medical imaging product based on a proprietary thermal process. This was followed by the Helios Laser Imaging System for the medical imaging market, film recorders and slides scanner series; LCD projectors and high resolution panels for computer imaging; and integrated electronic security and identification systems. In 1996, the first digital image camera was introduced and achieved unexpected market success. A whole series of digital cameras targeted for different segments followed. Polaroid has successfully and actively leveraged ecological forces to manage the process of formulating and implementing Polaroid strategy.

At Polaroid, there was a special emphasis by DiCamillo on expanding the pool of ideas about new strategic initiatives. He did this by encouraging everyone at Polaroid to contribute their ideas and allowing everyone to work on their own strategic initiatives, which so happened to be related to digital imaging. In fact only 40% of the projects were initiated by the senior management and most of the rest were started on suggestions from employees.

Next consider a story about 3M or Minnesota Mining and Manufacturing, the company widely known for its innovation. This story goes back some fifty years when a young employee called Dick Drew was visiting a car paint shop that was a customer of the company, and saw the trouble the workers had attempting to do the then in-vogue duo-tone paint-shop. He then went back to 3M and invented the masking tape. Five years later, he adapted the technology to come up with Scotch cellophane tape. The product has evolved into more than 900 varieties of pressure-sensitive tape alone. Again this was not in 3M's strategic plan. This was one of their first climbs in the fitness landscape and the company continues to jump to other peaks as the competition builds up and their fitness declines.

A similar incident occurred some 50 years later when another employee, Art Fry, was singing in a church and wondered if there were a way of making the slips of paper he used to mark his place in the hymn book stick to the page. Back at work his thought led him to look into the adhesive which he knew fellow employee Spencer Silver had been tinkering with as experiment. They soon came out with the idea of "Post It" notes which were an instant success. Again this was never in 3M's strategic plans. It all happened through the "Variation-Selection-Retention" process.

Honda's entry into the US motorcycle market is another example of strategy as a guided evolutionary process. In 1959 Honda sent a team of executives to the US to try to launch Honda's range of big motorcycles. This was part of their first step to capture the vast US market for big bikes. Some five years later, they did capture more than 60% of the market, but selling mostly small motorcycles instead. The whole thing started when the 50cc small motorcycle they brought to the US for their own use attracted more attention than their showcase models of larger bikes. This course of action built on some meetings with buyers from Sears, who saw the market opportunity for the products. From here Honda began to dominate the small motorcycle market in North America. Again, Honda's strategy was the result of "Variation-Selection-Retention" of strategic initiatives. Their success did not come from a predetermined strategic plan.

Contrary to accepted wisdom and the teachings of many business schools that strategy should be either vision-led or market-driven with a grand strategic plan tightly defining the firm's direction, activities and positions from "A" to "B," Sun's Java, 3M's Post It notes as well as many other cases of successful innovation, were all the results of autonomous and induced strategic initiatives or units, operating together to create the variation that the selective system operates. In Sun's case, the Java team was one of some twenty product teams working autonomously on different projects, all initiated by either an individual or a team in the organization. And their innovations were all induced, in the sense that the process "Variation-Selection-Retention" was guided by the strategic intent of McNealy. In 3M's case, the company harnessed more than 100 technologies which enabled them to create, develop and market more than 60,000 different products. And over time, this strategic intent will continuously be influenced by the strategic initiatives of any outcomes. This strategic redirection is a result of a guided evolutionary process which made previously peripheral competencies and knowledge more central to the evolution of the firm, finding new opportunities to leverage them. They constantly juggle between the three different strategic postures. This evolution also involves freeing up the use of resources to face discontinuities, followed by diffusing the results of organizational experimentation and innovation from the periphery of the organization to its core.

Sun's strategy based on Java has been achieved through steps such as identification and selection of products and technology, which led to innovations with high economies of scope. This allowed continuous repositioning as well as improved knowledge search, and evolution through strategic alliances with firms having complementary capabilities. The guided evolution process helped Sun dynamically maintain its competitive edge. Polariod's digital imaging business was also a result of variation, selection and retention of strategic initiatives. The guided evolution process fueled Polariod's corporate renewal, provided the innovation and freed Polaroid from a diminishing instant photography industry.

The concept of guided evolution can easily be found in many firms today, in particular in what I call multi-sectoral and multi-technology firms. There are two categories of this type of firm: One is when a firm moves into a field of technology close to its original field (e.g. Sun, Monsanto, Amgen, Applied Material) The other is the firm which integrates technologies in complex systems (e.g. Boeing, General Dynamics, BMW. Many of these companies are simultaneously positioned in several industries and operate in a number of large complex product-markets as well as geographic areas. Today's dynamic technology environment affects the way these firms define their business and strategy making process, and makes it almost impossible to define their competitive space. Traditional strategy concepts cannot offer much help for these firms to find their space against a backdrop of accelerating changes in non-specific and exogenous technologies that can be transformed to a considerable extent. This interaction of technologies undergoing rapid changes has created an environment characterized by uncertainty as well as by the advent of opportunities. The guided evolution concept can be a useful theory to help managers understand the process of strategy making and evolution and to what extent it is altered by ongoing discovery, learning and fusion of new knowledge and ideas.

Chapter 11

Practical lessons from the natural world

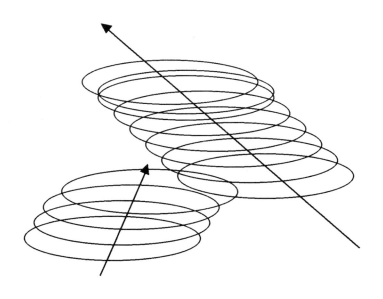

Practical lessons from the natural world

As we have discussed earlier in this book, much thinking and writing about strategy has remained in a world of hierarchy, stability and predictability. While we might be willing to embrace concepts such as "strategic intent" and "competing on capabilities" as promising alternatives, I think we have stopped far short of re-examining what these actually mean for the strategy development process in the real world, beyond just a general sense that strategic thinking deserves more attention. While we adopted the view of an organization as a living organism rather than a machine, we located the strategy making process as the "brain" inside our "heads" that was the senior management. That metaphor, I believe, is no longer useful for thinking about the process of strategy making. In strategy, the biggest mistake we have been making is the belief that we could somehow predict the future of our industries and that the future, a goal as a single point estimate, is predictable. Here I argue that it is not. Many organizations' most serious errors have occurred when they tried to tie strategies and plans rigidly to a set of assumptions about the future that later proved to be dead wrong. Our critical vulnerability has been an over confidence in our planning and analysis due to a lack of understanding of strategy tools. In addition, there has been a lack of awareness of the fact that the competencies that one organization possesses today may not be the critical factors in determining tomorrow's success. So not only is over-confidence in our ability to predict the future unwarranted; over-confidence in the adequacy of the current composition of our skills and values is equally dangerous.

Our critical vulnerability has been an **over-confidence** in our planning and analysis due to a lack of understanding of strategy tools.

Traditional strategic planning, like stock market analysis, fails to "Call the Turns," that is to identify important decisions that change the **dynamics** of a market.

Complexity theory can take us forward to a much more fundamental questioning of the role of intention in organizations, the very nature of management, control, and what we mean by strategic decision-making. It can open up a completely new approach to the whole industry and even the intra-organizational relationships within firms.

Comparing Different Strategy Concepts and Tools

	Porter	Hamel	D'Aveni	CAS
Industry Context	Low Complexity Relatively Stable	High Complexity Moderate Rate of Change	High Complexity High Rate of Change	High Complexity Super High Rate of Change
Strategy Concepts	Fit Strategy to Industry Structures	Competitive Innovation	Shift Rules of the Game	Managing at the Edge of Chaos
Primary Driver of Strategy	Strategy based on Competitive Analysis	Strategic Intent Stretch	Stakeholder Satisfaction	Fitness Landscape and Co-evolution
Basis of Competitive Advantage	Entry and Mobility Barriers	Core Competencies Leveraging	Speed and Surprise	Organizational Adaptability and Learning

An organization that successfully escapes velocity is one that constantly innovates and comes up with new solutions to old and new problems. When innovation is viewed from the perspective of complex adaptive system and complexity theory, we can see that innovation is the result of constructing strategies with a few simple but key elements which can constantly be experimented with and yet which produce results of a predictable kind in a predictable direction. That is not to say that they are predictable in the traditional sense, and this is an important distinction. We have borrowed the model from the formation of life and related it to the formation of business opportunities and directions. The next move in a strategic fitness landscape will be where there is a new combination of existing elements possible that takes only one new element to realize. A different form of organizational design can be helpful to provide a base for constant innovation. The requirements of organizational design for innovative and cognitive effectiveness are that a few basic design principles can be made explicit and then a number of various different models created from endless variations to match intentions with the environment. The key set of organizing principles is found in the following diagram:

By conceptualizing organizations as guided evolution systems a number of managerial implications can be developed. Long-term forecasting is almost impossible for these systems at the "edge of chaos," and dramatic change can occur unexpectedly; as a result, flexibility and adaptiveness are essential for organizations to survive. Nevertheless, the systems exhibit some degree of order, enabling short-term forecasting to be undertaken and underlying patterns to be discerned. It is important to develop guidelines and decision rules to cope with these complexities, and of search for non-obvious and indirect means to achieving goals. All of these call into question many of the traditions that have grown up around strategic planning with the tendency of treating strategic planning as operational planning without any disruption.

The journey in this book has led us to the four key conclusions:

First, many assumptions currently applied in management and organization theory and practice have led to a situation where firms seem unable to continuously adapt to their own environments. Complex adaptive systems theory offers an alternative set of assumptions with which to construct a new theory of organizational adaptation.

Critical to an organization's ability to reap the benefits of the complex adaptive systems approach, is its ability to surface and unlearn its dominant logic. Developing a capacity to work with mental models involve both seeing things through new lenses, learning new skills, and implementing institutional innovations that help bring these skills into practice. Institutionalizing the process of reflecting on and surfacing dominant logic requires the development of mechanisms that make these practices unavoidable. This could mean recasting traditional strategic planning as a learning mode. And corporate planning as institutional learning. In this process, senior management teams exchange their shared mental models of their company and their planning process then becomes learning process.

The learning skills needed to develop and manipulate dominant logic fall into two classes: skills of reflection and skills of inquiry. Skills of reflection enable us to slow our thinking process so that we can become more sensitive and aware of how our dominant logic came about and in what ways it influences our actions and behaviors. Inquiry skills and concerned with how we operate in face-to-face interactions with others, especially in dealing with complex issues that could lead to conflict. This includes asking ourselves such questions as how one believes the world works - the nature of business, who are our customers, how do we create value etc. Then ask yourself where these assumptions come from and are you willing to consider them inaccurate or even totally misleading. It is very important to ask these questions consciously because if the answer is no, there is no point in moving forward. Then the next step is to question these assumptions and generalizations and explicitly separate them from the data that led to their formation. Try testing this directly and it may lead to inquiring into the reasons behind each individual's action. When advocating one's view of logic, the best way to do it is to make your reasoning explicit and encourage others to explore your view as well as provide different views.

Second, changing assumptions is simply not enough: firms obviously also need to act differently. Organizations must climb and explore, develop knowledge and recognize patterns, co-evolve with other organizations, and organize internally to reflect the blend of stability and chaos that exists on their own competencies and knowledge landscape.

> Don't just **think** differently; also **act** differently. We need to attack and at the same time make a good defense, maintaining the delicate balance between survival and advancement.

Stacey (1992) notes that systems, like organizations, are most creative when they operate away from equilibrium, in a region of "Creative Tension". He suggests that leaders work to create a "space for creativity", and attempt to contain - but not eliminate - the "anxiety" of their co-workers. Such "creative chaos" Nonaka (1988, 1995) may need to be intentionally created by senior management through a deliberate "fluctuation" to dissolve an existing order that exists in the organization, and allow for self-organization processes. Nonaka further cautions that if managers are not allowed time for reflection during this time, creative chaos can become "destructive chaos", so he proposes redundancy be built into managerial structures and processes. In a similar vein, Zimmerman (1993) argues that rather than attempting to absorb uncertainty, managers should recognize the evolutionary need to expand uncertainty as humans have "limitless ability to create connections." Zimmerman and Hurst (1993) propose that this might involve thinking about the fractal nature of organizational boundaries. In this light, senior management should realize that all employees are at some boundary of their organizations, and therefore understand part of their firm's environment.

Arthur (1990, 1996) asserts there are really two economies, one in which traditional diminishing returns function, and the other, including most knowledge industries, where increasing returns to scale are evident due to positive feedback. Trade theory and corporate strategy should take increasing returns into account, including understanding the risks of being "locked in" through positive feedback to an inferior technology or path of development. In an environment where cause-effect relationships are tenuous at best, managers need to look for interrelationships and patterns rather than conduct forecasting based on rationalist causes and effects (Senge, 1990; Levy, 1994). In the knowledge economy, companies should focus on adapting, recognizing patterns, and building webs to amplify positive feedback rather than trying to achieve "optimal" performance. Companies and economies need to be structured to encourage self-organizing evolution (Stacey 1992).

Jantsch (1980) describes the co-evolutionary process that takes place between an organization and its environment, advocating an evolutionary approach to planning rather than a rational one. He recognizes such an approach will likely lead to increase management uncertainty, but supports this as beneficial.

From the point of view of complexity and of the cognitive nature of business, the continued dramatic expansion of information processing and exchanging technology is changing the competitive landscape far more dramatically and rapidly than machines did during the industrial revolution. This technology increase is what makes the current research into complex adaptive systems possible as well as new approaches to organization and processes of doing business. At a recent "complexity" conference, business challenges were addressed by Colin Crook of CitiBank, John Chambers of Cisco, and John Seely Brown of Xerox. Surprisingly the focus of each was not on the technology itself but rather on how technology was affecting the way that we organize to do business. Large and historically successful businesses are not organized to deal with the rapid change and new models demanded by changes in technology. Technology demands these changes - more accurately, competitors' adaptation to new technology demands it - but the key problem is that the major shift in thinking that is required to use the technology are not provided by the technology itself. But new kinds of dialogue have since become possible using technology such as the web, Lotus Notes and other new applications. Not only can dialogue be distributed over time and space but there are unique features possible due to saving and navigation of conversations as well as those made possible by constructed demands on time delay and memory.

Third, the traditional microeconomics model assumes that value will accrue to organizations that possesses structural advantages over their competitors. In many industry sectors, this still holds true. But very often "competitive advantage" can be built on other foundations such as industry foresights or insights. The pace and unpredictability of change have rendered strategies based on narrowly focused definitions of products and markets inflexible and vulnerable. This is a shift in the focus of strategic planning from products and markets to capabilities. Capabilities analysis, however, is complicated by the rapid disintegration of the traditional industry boundaries that once drew the dividing lines between firms and businesses. We have heard many times the idea of "The End of Industries" as we all know them.

Consider the case of personal financial services, where the collapse of barriers between the previously distinct banking, insurance, stock brokerages and financial planning is reshaping the competitive space. The same has happened in the telecom industry, where again the collapse of barriers between the previously distinct entertainment, news media, cable and data communications is reshaping the competitive landscape. Here I propose a further shift in the focus of strategy making from capabilities or core competencies to competencies-and-knowledge-landscapes. The competencies and knowledge may lie in either scientific or processes management expertise, management creativity and innovation, or the ability to manage strategic alliances from customers to suppliers. In this new world, competencies and knowledge landscapes are at the heart of business strategy.

Map out your "Competencies and Knowledge" landscape and constantly look out for changes. Remember this is a constant battle in the market between the **order** of things, and established players **defending** their future cash flows.

Under the complex adaptive systems paradigm, the manager's role is to monitor the organization's competencies and fitness and the ever-changing landscape while looking out for the next peak to hop.

Fourth, the traditional model makes assumptions that uncertainty is quite low in an industry and that a company can make reasonably accurate predictions on which to base its strategy. Some managers even pretend that uncertainty does not exist at all. The new model we discuss here assumes that uncertainty is high and it not realistic to make any meaningful predictions on which to base strategy. The secret of strategy making lies in the ability to determine the level of certainty in any industry and tailor strategies using different approaches to cater to that degree of uncertainty. Michael Porter(1998) wrote in a Harvard Business Review article that developing a strategy in a new industry or in a business undergoing revolutionary technological changes is a daunting proposition.

Managers face a higher level of uncertainty about needs of customers, the products and services that will prove to be most desired, and the best configuration of activities and technologies to deliver them. During such periods in an industry's development, its basic productivity frontier is being established or reestablished. A period of imitation may be inevitable in emerging industries, but the period reflects the level of uncertainty rather than a desired state of affairs. And in high-tech industries, this imitation phase often continues much longer than it should. This is a realistic description of industry evolution and coincides with the illustrations of "punctuated equilibrium."

In an environment where uncertainty is high, managers need a profoundly different approach to goal-setting. My main argument is, would it be wise to adopt a rigid goal in the early stages of a game when probably no one knows how the industry will develop or evolve? It is true that from the outset we need a general direction: if particular actions are not informed by an overall conception, behavior will respond only to the demand of the moment. And to propel the organization out of the imitation phase, goals may need to be made specific and articulated. But, in the new fast-evolving industries of the knowledge economy, where major players can shape the game and shift the rules and new players can emerge, a rigid definition of the final goals too early in the game can blind us in the course of development and limit our flexibility.

Using a traditional strategic planning process in a **fast** changing sector will resemble a 40 year old trying to win Wimbledon with a wooden racket

One way out of this dilemma is set intermediate goals according to the criterion of maximum "Efficiency Diversity." A situation is characterized by high efficiency diversity if it offers many possibilities for action that have relatively higher probability of success. To cope with the lack of clarity inherent in complex systems, we need to "deconstruct" them. It brings clarity. And along with it difficulties, for often after we have analyzed a complex system in this way there has no single "center". Two key elements are continuous improvement and the learning mindset, so dominant in discussions of high performance, and the need to experiment in order to achieve. No longer do we expect to get it right the first try. We can learn from our mistakes. As a result, we have begun to pay serious attention to the idea of organizational learning and the potential offered by the "learning" organizations. As Tom Peters puts it in "Liberation Management:" "Success in the marketplace today is directly proportional to the knowledge that an organization can bring to bear, how fast it can bring that knowledge to bear, and the rate at which it accumulates knowledge."

Complex Adaptive Systems Strategy Approach

Local Peaks

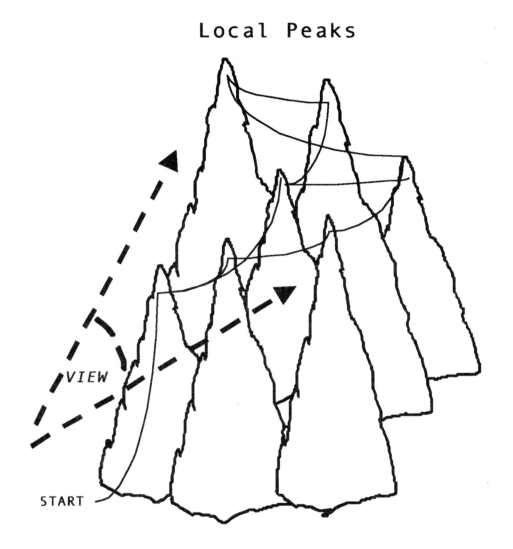

Think about learning from venture capitalists like setting **multiple** intermediate goals according to the criterion of maximum "Efficiency Diversity."

One key principle of complex adaptive system is that once a company reaches a temporary "peak" in its fitness landscape, **it must first go down to go up**. In cybernetic terms, the organism must be pulled by competitive pressures far enough out of its usual arrangements before it can create substantially different forms and arrive at an evolved basin of attraction.

A **thought** in closing

This book provides only partial answers to the many questions of "strategy." Further research is necessary to help answer some of the most important questions facing organizational and management scholars today; how environments and context can shape organizations, and how "guided" organizational evolution depends on history, experience, and interrelationships between the organization and its environment. Complexity theory challenges our existing views of strategy and shifts our thinking away from "steady state" concepts like vision, missions, leadership and core businesses, and focuses on processes and organizational dynamics at the expense of content and analysis. It emphasizes the necessity for experimentation in strategy, but critically it also underlines the importance of revolutionary changes in business logic and competitive behavior.

As Stephen Hawking (1997) suggests, the world is on the edge of another major discontinuity, with the ability to manipulate our DNA pulling humanity into a new phase of "...self-designed evolution...." How successfully organizations and social institutions can be reshaped will have profound consequences for future generations. No amount of personal or interpersonal skills will ever be sufficient, if the organizational practices are not founded on science. We would do well to remember the words of Leonardo Da Vinci who noted that, "Those who are obsessed with practice, but have no science, are like a pilot setting out with no tiller or compass, who will never know for certain where he is going." This book proposes a science of organizations and strategy based on a much deeper, systems understanding of our natural world; enabling us to organize simply for complexity. I believe this new theoretical framework can help us address some of the pressing challenges of organization that our world faces now and into the next millennium.

> "Those who are obsessed with practice, but have no science, are like a pilot setting out with no tiller or compass, who will **never** know for certain where he is going."
>
> Leonardo Da Vinci

Einstein once said that no problem could be solved from the same consciousness that created it. You have to step out of what you are currently thinking in order to see things differently. We need to stand back and ask the question: Is there a simpler way to manage the complexity of modern organizations given the turbulent environment which is here to stay? Look at almost any large multi-national corporation anywhere in the world and you will find that it is based on some strong assumptions of the world as a machine. In a machine, you have separate parts. They have to be well tooled; they're replaceable. You can't tolerate change with a machine; you want a stable environment. That mentality led us to create organizations based on what I call 17th-century assumptions about the world as a machine. What we're seeing today is really the death of 17th-century models. The meaning of organization has dramatically over the last ten years. A entity that was once primarily formal and physical has evolved into something informal, non-material and altogether more fluid. And we are looking to a future, whether we like it or not, in which we will not be shored up by rigid structures and strategies, because they don't work any more. Disorder creates losers, but it also create winners. If it is seen as an opportunity, then the greater the rate of disorder, the more opportunities to win there will be. Guided evolution can give us insights into whether complexity metaphors - fitness landscapes, edge of chaos, path dependence, punctuated equilibrium, increasing returns - when accepted into the vocabulary of an organization, can change both the way managers manage and the problems they choose to manage. If this phenomenon proves to hold true, perhaps there really is need a to reconsider important precepts of many existing strategic management theories.

> "Our thinking creates problems which the same level of thinking **can't** solve."
>
> Einstein

Business is a cognitive activity of the enterprise. It is not sufficient to have brilliant people designing great strategies. We must enhance the ability of the organization as a whole to sense, interpret and choose processes which are generative. What we need to develop is the organizational intelligence. Intelligence is a function of the organization of the connections between cells, their elements, and the larger systems that they are part of. These connections are iterative and mutually influencing at all times. The organization of the corporation, like the organization of all living things is primarily a matter of relationship, communication, connections and responsiveness. Organizing to develop organizational intelligence is about the organization of communication and relationships that enhance the information processing, in its broadest sense, of the whole. Unlike other living systems, however, in corporate organization we have some important unique features: firstly, we have an influence on our particular organization structure, and secondly, the primary element being organized is linguistic or language based. It is the flow of words and their meaning that is important in corporate organization. Hence we have a great deal to say about our own organization designs. Complexity theory not only provides concepts but also a language to assist in new designs for our organizations of the future.

Fundamental theories of business and strategy are under constant attack, as Peter Drucker tells in his book "The Theory of Business" - and to survive, managers must learn to swiftly shift behaviors in their organizations to exploit new theories and assumptions about business and strategy.

I believe that, like many other tools in this world, most of these concepts are appropriate only in specific situations within a broader picture. Managers, executives and strategists need to have a deep understanding of many concepts and tools, without bias toward any one of them. In my view, strategy making is a process of continuous adaptation that straddles the tension between offering too much or too little direction; between collaborating to create new value systems and competing for a larger piece of the piece; between reaping the benefits of autonomy and losing the benefits of scale and scope; and between relying too heavily on or disrupting too precipitously the status quo.

In toady's diverse business conditions, we must take into account a much wider range of industry structures and bases of competition. Many strategy theories developed during the last thirty years look narrowly at the industry competitive dynamics and the comparing of profits between competitive firms. Their plain focus on value appropriation is due to their deep preconception that the success of a firm must be at the expense of other firms or even the social welfare of society. But innovative strategies that are capable of value creation will result in more value being created and transferred to more firms and society at large. And that's what I call economic progress.

Traditional business strategy, like stock market analysis, fails to "Call the Turns," that is to identify important decisions that change the dynamics of a market. However, in management, there is always a danger that "faddism" will take over before the implications of which "complexity theory" has been properly digested.

There has been a lot of hype about the science of "complexity theory" but we must understand it is not "theories for everything."

Expanded Framework of Strategy Making Concepts

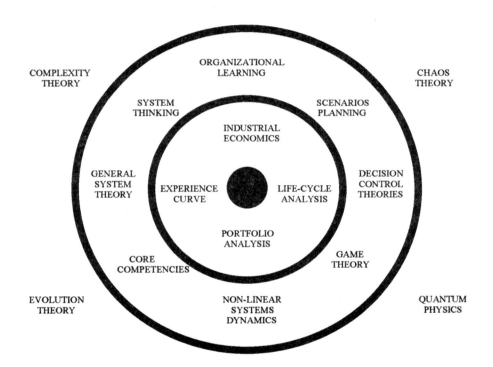

glossary

Cellular Automata
Introduced by American mathematician Jon von Neuman and Stanislaw W. Ulam, cellular automata is a mathematical model of physical phenomena which is based on the idea of an array of cells, each of which represent an automation or abstract machine which takes on a finite number of states. Each cell is simple but together the system is capable of complex behavior.

Chaos Theory
The study of phenomena which appear random, but in fact have an element of regularity which can be described mathematically. Chaotic behavior has been found to exist in a wide range of applications, such as seizures or pelisses, atmospheric prediction models and fibrillation of the heart.

Co-Evolution
When at least two agents evolve together over time, and one adapts to selection pressures imposed by the other, they are said to co-evolve. Agents in co-evolving systems interact, with some forming niches that allow the existence of others in loose hierarchies or "food webs"

Complexity Theory
The attempted classification according to difficulty of algorithms and computational methods, often for problems in Combinatorics or Optimization Theory. The study of how and why large systems

behave in ways unexplainable by the sum of their parts. Free markets are probably the best example of complex adaptive systems. The theory originated from the study of the natural environment; it also helps to explain how feedback loops can cause systems to stall.

Darwinism
The term coined by British naturalist Alfred Russel Wallace after the eminent evolutionary theorist Charles Darwin. Darwin's original hypothesis holds that individuals possessing characteristics enabling them to produce more viable offspring than less well-endowed individuals, will tend to have those characteristics maintained and spread throughout the population via natural selection.

Dynamic System Theory
A way of describing a process that constantly changes over time, such as internal combustion in an engine or the movement of the financial markets. This theory holds that any change in one part of dynamic system influences all interrelated parts. It finds particular favor in the psychology of groups.

Equilibrium Theory
Economic body of analysis examining the balance of related variables of an economy and their tendency to resist change. Classic economic theory, outlined by Scottish economist Adam Smith, regarded market prices as fluctuating around the natural price trend. The French economist Leon Walras developed a theory of general equilibrium, in which all markets of an economy are studied, and in which all supplies, prices and outputs of goods and factors are determined simultaneously.

Emergence

Agents in complex adaptive systems self-regulate and mutually adjust, with new forms of order becoming apparent over time. No central direction is evident. The process by which local actions by agents leads to the formation of patterns or structures on a global level is known as emergence, which is also related to Holland's property of aggregation.

Fractals

The term "fractal" was coined by Polish born American mathematician Benoit Mandelbrot to describe a feature of his Mandelbrot sets, in which any part of the set magnified was found to contain elements of the whole. Fractals are self-similar, meaning they have similar but not identical structures on all scales.

Genetic Algorithm

Adam Smith's invisible hand joined with Darwin's principle of natural selection, inside a computer. Components of a highly complex problem are broken down into building blocks, whose characteristics are represented in code. During a computer simulation, the units of code then recombine with each other to make offspring, just like parents' genes combine in children. The best offspring are then allowed to reproduce again. As generations go on, better and better code evolves, which is then translated back into objects in the real world.

Natural Selection
Also known as the survival of the fittest. Its importance was first recognized by the Charles Darwin and it is the concept that the genetic component of individuals with superior characteristics for survival and reproduction will eventually overcome that of individuals less well endowed individuals. Natural selection is the key mechanism for Darwinian evolution.

Non-linear
A description in which effects are totally out of proportion to causes, so that a small change in a variable can have enormous consequences or, conversely, a huge change has little effect. Many scientists believe that nature was neither linear or non-linear, but a hybrid of both plus noises that no intellectual system can conquer or manage.

Positive Feedback
When a deviation exists between the expectation and the outcome of a system, negative feedback processes lead the gap to shrink and eventually disappear. However, positive or amplifying feedback, causes the gap to expand. The original deviation is thus magnified rather than reduced.

Self-Organized Criticality
Complex systems naturally evolve to a critical state, where a minor event can begin a chain reaction which cascades through the system. Conducting an experiment by dropping single grains of sand on to a sandpile, Bak and Chen (1991) found that the frequency and magnitude of avalanches follows a power law, that is, there is a systematic relationship between large and small avalanches. For example, for every avalanche involving 100 grains of sand, there will

have been 1000 avalanches involving one grain of sand. The theory has been used variously to explain the extinction of the dinosaurs, stock market crashes, and forest fires.

Sensitive Dependency on Initial Conditions
Also referred to as the "butterfly effect", SDIC is the phrase used to describe the phenomena that undetectable differences in starting conditions can lead complex systems, through a series of bifurcations, to vastly different endpoints.

Strange Attractors
Unlike "point" attractors - spots to which a system such as a pendulum gravitates as it moves towards equilibrium - "strange" attractors are a range or zone of different points to which a system is attracted. Almost no matter what the initial conditions, the system will move towards and be bounded by the attractor.

references

Anderson, P.W., Arrow, K.J., and Pines (1988) The Economy as an Evolving Complex System. Addison-Wesley, Redwood City, CA.
Aoki, M. (1996) New Approaches to Macroeconomics Modeling: Evolutionary Stochastic Dynamics and Multiple Equilibria. Cambridge Univeristy Press, New York.
Argyris, C. and Schon, D. (1978) Organizational Learning: A Theory of Action Perspective, Addison-Wesley, Reading.
Arthur, W.B. (1990) Positive Feedbacks in the Economy, Scientific American, February.
Arthur, W.B. (1993) On the Evolution of Complexity, paper presented at Stanford University, April 11.
Arthur, W.B. (1996) Increasing Returns and New World of Business, Harvard Business Review, July-August
Ansoff, I.H. (1965) Corporate Strategy, McGraw Hill, New York.
Bateson, G. (1979) Mind and Nature: A Necessary Unity. Bantam Books, New York.
Berk, C. and F. Schlogl (1993) Thermodynamics of Chaotic Systems. Cambridge University Press, Cambridge.
Berreby, David (1998) Complexity Theories : Fact-free Science of Business Tools, Strategy and Business Issue 10
Berreby, David (1996) Strategy and Business: What Complexity Theory can teach Business. Issue 3.
Bettis, R. and Prahalad, C.K. (1995) The Dominant Logic: Retrospective and Extension, Strategic Management Journal, Vol.16
Blanchard, G. (1992) Business Strategy for the New Europe. European Trends.
Bower, J.L. (1970) Managing the Resource Allocation Model, Harvard University, Boston.
Burns T. and Stalker, G. (1961) The Management of Innovation, Tavistock, London.
Burt. R. (1992) Structural Holes : The Social Structure of Competition. Harvard Business School Press, Cambridge.
Chandler, A.D. (1962) Strategy and Structure, MIT Press, Cambridge.
Chandler, A.D. (1990) The Enduring Logic of Industrial Success. Harvard Business Review Mar-Apr.
Choi, Y. B., (1993). Paradigms and Conventions: Uncertainty, Decision making, and Entrepreneurship. University of Michigan Press, Ann Arbor.
Cyert, R.M. and March, J.G. (1963) A Behavioral Theory of the Firm, Englewood Cliffs, Prentice Hall, New Jersey.
Cyert, R.M. and Williams J.R. (1993) Organizations, Decision Making and Strategy: Strategic Management Journal, Special Issue (Winter)
D'Aveni, R.A. (1994) Hyper Competition, The Free Press, New York.
De Geus, A. (1995). Remarks to "Complexity and Strategy: The Intelligent Organization" Conference, London, May.
Drucker, P.F. (1993) Post-Capitalist Society, Butterworth Heinemann, London.

Edvinsson, L. and Sullivan, P. (1996) Developing a Model for Managing Intellectual Capital, European Management Journal, Vol 14 No 4, August.

Eigen, M. and Oswatitsch, R.W. (1992) Steps Towards Life: A Perspective on Evolution, Oxford University Press., New York.

Ghoshal, S, and Lovas B. (1997) Strategy as Guided Evolution, London Business School Working Paper

Gleick, J. (1987). Chaos, Viking, New York.

Hamel, G. (1989) Strategic Intent, Harvard Business Review Mar/Apr Boston

Hamel, G. (1993) Strategy as Stretch and Leverage, Harvard Business Review Mar/Apr Boston

Hamel, G. and Prahalad. C.K. (1994) Competing for the Future, Harvard Business School Press, Boston.

Hammer, M. and Champy, J. (1990) Re-Engineering the Corporation: A Manifesto for Business Revolution. Nicholas Brealey, London.

Handy, C. (1989) The Age of Unreason, Random House, London.

Hill, R. C. and M. Levenhagen, (1995). Metaphors and Mental Models: Sense-making and Sense-giving in Innovation . Journal of Management.

Holland, J. (1995). Hidden Order. Addison-Wesley, Reading, Mass.

Horgan, J. (1995). From Complexity to Perplexity, Scientific American, June

Johnson, J.L. and Burton, B.K. (1994) Chaos and Complexity Theory for Management: Journal of Managerial Inquiry, Vol. 3 No. 4, Dec

Kauffman, S. (1991) Antichaos and Adaptation, Scientific American. Aug

Kauffman, S. (1993) The Origins of Order: Self-Organization and Selection in Evolution. Oxford University Press, New York.

Kauffman, S. (1995) At Home in the Universe. Viking, London.

Kauffman, S. (1995) Technology and Evolution: Escaping the Red Queen Effect, The McKinsey Quarterly, No.1.

Kelly, K. (1994) Out of Control: The Rise of Neo-Biological Civilization, Addison-Wesley, Reading, Mass.

Lakoff, G. and Johnson, M. (1995). Metaphors We Live By, University of Chicago Press, Chicago.

Langton, C.G.,Taylot,C.,Farmer,J.D. and Rasmussen S. (1992) Artificial Life II. Addison-Wesley, Redwood City.

Lawrence, P.R. and Lorsch, J.W. (1967) Organization and Environment,: Harvard Business School, Boston

Leonard-barton, D. (1992) Core Capabilities and Core Rigidities, Strategic Management Journal, Vol. 13.

Levy, D. (1994) Chaos Theory and Strategy: Theory, Application and Managerial Implications, Strategic Management Journal, Vo.15.

Lewin. R. (1993) Complexity: Life on the Edge of Chaos, Orion Books, London.

Lane, D. and Maxfield, R., (1995). Foresight Complexity and Strategy, Santa Fe Institute Working Papers,

Lorenz, E. (1963) Deterministic Nonperiodic Flow, Journal of Atmospheric Sciences No. 20.

March, J.G. and Simon, H. (1958) Organizations, Wiley, New York.

Meyer, A.D., Boorks, G. and Goes, J. (1990) Environmental Jolts and Industry Revolutions: Organizational Responses to Discontinuous Change. Strategic Management Journal.
Miller, S. and Friesen, P.H. (1984) Organizations: A Quantum Review, Prentice Hall, New Jersey.
Mintzberg, H. (1987) Crafting Strategy, Harvard Business Review (Jul/Aug) Boston
Mintzberg, H. (1994) The Rise and Fall of Strategic Planning, Harvard Business Review (Jan/Feb)) Boston
Morgan, G. (1986) Images of Organization, Sage, Newbury Park.
Moore, J.K. (1993) Predators and Prey: A New Ecology of Competition. Harvard Business Review (May-Jun)
Nicolis, G. and Prigogine, I. (1977) Self-Organization in Nonequilibrium System: From Dissipative Structures to Order through Fluctuations.: John Wiley, New York.
Nonaka, I. and Takeuchi, H. (1995) The Knowledge-Creating Company, Oxford University Press, Oxford.
Nonaka, I. (1994). A Dynamic Theory of Organizational Knowledge Creation. Organization Science
Parker, D. and Stacey, R. (1994) Chaos, Management and Economics: The Implications of Non-Linear Thinking, Hobart Paper 125, London.
Pettigrew, A. ed. (1987) The Management of Strategic Change, Basil Blackwell, Oxford.
Peters, T. (1988) Thriving on Chaos, Macmillan, New York.
Phelan, S., (1995) From Chaos to Complexity in Strategic Planning, paper presented to the Academy of Management
Prahalad, C.K. and Bettis, R.A. (1986) The Dominant Logic: A New Linkage between Diversity and Performance, Strategic Management Journal, Vol. 7.
Porter, M. E. (1980) Competitive Strategy, Free Press, New York.
Porter, M. E. (1985) Competitive Advantage, Free Press, New York.
Porter, M. E. (1987) The State of Strategic Planning, Economist, May.
Porter, M.E. (1996) What is Strategy, Harvard Business Review, Nov/Dec 1996, Boston.
Schein, E.H. (1985) Organizational Culture and Leadership: A Dynamic View, Jossey Bass, San Francisco.
Schumpeter, J.A. (1951) Economic Theory and Entrepreneurship History, Addison-Wesley, Cambridge.
Schumpeter, J.A. (1991) The Study of Entrepreneurship, Princeton University Press, New Jersey.
Senge, P. (1990) The Fifth Discipline: The Art and Practice of the Learning Organization. Random House, Boston.
Simon, H. (1989) Models of Thought, Vol. 2, Yale University Press, New Haven, Conn.
Simon, H. (1993) Strategy and Organizational Evolution, Strategic Management Journal, Special Issue Winter.
Southern, G. (1994) Introducing Business Process Re-Engineering: A Brainstorming Approach. Business Change and Re-Engineering, Summer.
Stacey, R. (1992) Managing Chaos, Kogan-Page, London.
Stacey, R. (1995) The Science of Complexity: An Alternative Perspective for Strategic Change Processes, Strategic Management Journal, Vol. 16.

Stacey, R. (1996) Complexity and Creativity in Organizations, Barrett-Koehler, San Francisco.
Strebel, P. (1992) Breakpoints: How Managers Exploit Radical Business Change, Harvard Business School Press, Boston.
Strebel, P.,and Volikangas, L.(1994) Organizational Change Processes in a Force Field. International Review of Strategic Management, Vol. 5 John Wiley, New York.
Sveiby, K.E. (1996) Transfer of Knowledge and the Information Processing Professions, European Management Journal, Vol. 14, No. 4 .
Thompson, J.D. (1967) Organizations in Action, McGraw Hill, New York.
Sullivan G. and Harper M. (1996) Hope is not a Method, Random House, New York
Tushman, M.L. and Anderson, P. (1986) Technological Discontinuities and Organization Environments, Administrative Science Quarterly 31
Varela, F., Thompson, E., Rosch, E. (1991) The Embodied Mind, MIT Press, Cambridge.
Waldrop, M.M. (1992). Complexity: The Emerging Science at the Edge of Chaos. Simon & Schuster, New York.
Vinten, G. (1992) Thriving on Chaos, Management Decision 30.
Vriend, N.J. (1994) Self-organized Markets in a Decentralized Economy , Working Paper, Sante Fe Institute
Wheatley, M. (1992) Leadership and the New Science: Learning about Organization from an Orderly Universe. Berrett-Koehler, San Francisco.
Wolfram. S. (1996) Theory and Applications of Cellular Automata. World Scientific. Singapore.
Zimmerman, B. (1992) Chaos and Self-Renewing Organizations: Designing Transformation Processes for Co-Evolution. Faculty of Administration Studies, York University, Working Paper, May.
Zimmerman, B. (1993) The Inherent Drive Towards Chaos, Implementing Strategic Processes, Blackwell, Oxford.
Zimmerman, B. and Hurst, D. (1993) Breaking the Boundaries: The Fractal Organization, Journal of Management Inquiry, Vol. 2.

index

Adaptive Walls 120
Agents 97
Agent-based Models 75
Alfred Sloan Jr. 42
Amaon.com 54, 125
Amgen 141
Amos Tuck School of Business 37
Anderson, Phil 68
Anderson Consulting 37
Andrew, Ken 30, 43
Ansoff 40
Applied Material 141
Apple 36, 42, 100
Arms races 85
Arrow, Kenneth 68, 69
Arthur, Brian 68, 69
Artifacts 18
Ashby 81
AT&T 102
Arms Race 81
Amgen 134
Australia 89
Applied Material 135

Barnes and Noble 125
BCG 43
Blue sky brainstorming 19
Bell Atlantic 126
Berners-Lee 89
Bettis and Prahalad 41
Boeing 141
Boston Consulting Group 30
BMW 141
Breathing 23

Building B locks 71
Burns and Stalker 21

Capacity Utilization 31
Cargill 133
Carroll, Lewis 84
Cellular Automata 61, 62, 96, 100, 160
CNN 54
Chandler, Alfred 21, 42
Christensen, C. Roland 30
Chaos Theory 39, 61, 160
Chaotic Systems 12
Chiron Corp. 136
Ciba Geigy 111
Class I models 65,
Class II models 65
Class III models 65
Class IV models 65
Climbing Local Peaks 121
Comdisco 75
Complex Adaptive Systems Theory 23
Consultants News 31
Corporate Strategy 27
Central Evolutionary and Transformational Processes 20
Cisco 127, 128
Citibank 102
Coca-Cola 102
Competing on capability 143
Complex Adaptive Systems 20, 69
Complexity Theory 62
Core Capability 120

Core Competencies 29
Corporate Strategy 28
Creative Chaos 150
Critical Resource 29
Complex Dynamic Systems 40, 61, 62
Cognitive 11, 70, 71, 141
Coupling 90, 117
Cyert and March 21

Da Vinci, Leonardo 160
Darwinian 8, 9
Darwin, Charles 77, 78
DEKALP Genetics Corp. 123
Doctrine of management 8, 10
Dominant logic 41
D'Aveni 37, 38
Deliberate Choices 34
Dell computers 54
Destructive chaos 150
Desert Storm 4
DiCamillo, Gary 137
Diversity 70, 86
Drew, Dick 162
Drucker, Peter 17, 162
Dynamic of Fitness Improvement 120
Diminishing returns 35, 146

eBay 54
Ecles Robert
Economies of Scale 34
Edge of Chaos 66, 92, 100, 129, 147
Efficiency Diversity 156
Einstein 161
Error Catastrophe 93

Error Threshold 93
Errisson 128
Eigen and Oswatitsch 93
Epistatic coupling 94
Exploring the Landscape 121
Extended transients 65
Exxon 102
Evolutionary Theory 11, 75, 77

Fry, Art 138
France 16
Feel-good 22
Fit to stretch 38
Fitness Landscape 93
Flows 70
Ford 102
Friesen 20

Gale of Creative Destruction 5
Game of Life 64
Gell-Mann, Murray 93
General Dynamics 141
General Motors 15, 42
Genetic variety 36
Geneticists 94
Germany 16
Ghoshal, Sumatra 9
Grand plan 36
Great minds 36
Grove-in 36
Guided Evolution 115
Guerillas 4

Hamel and Prahalad 36, 37, 38, 120
Hamel, Gary 25, 26, 115

Handy, Charles 6, 4
Harvard Business School 27, 28
Harvard Business Review 154
Hawking, Stephen 159
Heisenberg, Werner 106, 107
Henderson, Bruce 31
Helios Laser Imaging System 137
HIV 111
Home Depot 100
Holland, John 68
Honda 139
Hong Kong 89
Hotmail.com 54
HMV 125

IBM 15, 42, 100
ICI 102
Ikea 54
Internal White Space 2
Internal Models 71
Inter-relationships 34
Irving Fisher 35
Industry breakpoints 4
Industrial Revolution 83
In Search of Excellence 15

Jantsch 151
Java 135 - 140
Japan 16
Johnson and Burton 71
Johnson and Johnson 102

Killer Product 7
Killer Application 7

Knowledge Management 7
Kodak 102
Korea 16
Knowledge economy 11, 17, 114, 122, 146, 150

Land's End 100
Lawrence 21
Leonard-Barton 120
Law of Requisite Variety 81
Lawrence and Lorsch 21
Levy 151
Lewin Roger 23
Leon Walras 35
Lotus 100
Lorsh 21
Little, D. Arthur 31
Locked in 151
London Business School 9
Lorenz 63
Lucent, 128
Levy 146

3M 102, 138
Mac 36
Management Doctrine 9
Marshall, Alfred 35, 50, 52, 53
McDonald 102
Metaphorical models 16
Menger, Carl 31
Microsoft 36, 125, 126
Miller and Friesen 21
Minnesota Mining and Manufacturing 138
Mintzberg 21, 40, 41
Monsanto 132, 135

Muddling through 43
Muray Gell-Mann 68
McNealy, Scott 135 - 141
Monte Carlo 72

Neuman, Jon Von 64
New 7s Framework 37
Nicolis and Prigogine 63
Nobel laureate Ilya Prigogine 53
Nonaka 150
Nohria, Nitin 22
Non-equilibrium system 53
Non-linearity 70
Nortel 128
Netscape 100, 125, 126
Newtonian 20, 23, 71

Options writers 114
Outside the box 19
Oswatitsch 89

Paul Romer 72
Path Dependence 100
PECO Energy 36
Pentagon 4
Pettigrew 21
Peter, L 90
Peter Principle 90, 91
Peters, Tom 15, 156
Polariod 136, 137
Population of one 79
Porter, Michael 29, 32, 57
Plant Breeding Int'l Cambridge Ltd. 133
PriceWaterhouseCoopers 74

Primordial soup 87
Process 2, 13, 16
Puncuated Equilbrium 67, 99, 155
Purposeless organizations 43 X
Prahalad 34, 36, 40, 116, 172
Prigogine, Ilya 53
Prigogine 47

Red Queen 84, 91, 98, 127
Resource-based View 119
Rockfeller, JD 80

Scenario Planning 106
Schumpeter 4, 57
Selectivity 26
Strategic Planning 21, 27, 39, 40-44, 97
Stretch 140
Santa Fe Institute 68, 69
Schumpeter 4, 58
Sears 100, 139
Senge 151
Shapers 113
Shell 102
Silicone Graphics 100
Silicon Valley 100
Snapshot analysis 57
Southern 22
Southwest Airlines 54
Spirals of innovation 88
Stacey 20, 66, 150, 151
Stalins, Joe 2
Stanley, William 31
Strategic adapter 97
Strategic Intent 143
Sun Microsystems 100

Sweden 16
System intervention 22

Tagging 70
Technology-blind Strategies 37
Technology and Competitive
Strategy 29
Tele-CommunicationsInc. 126
The End of Industries 153
Thompson 21
Towers Records 125
3Ms 97, 133, 134
Theories for Everything 158
TQM 28

University of Michigan 69
Unix 135
US Army 10

Vriend 97
Valen, L van 84
Variation-Selection-Retenion 139
Value Appropriation 26, 93, 118, 157
Value Creation 7, 118, 157
Value chain 16, 32, 33

Walras, Levy 31
Wal-mart 100
Walfdrop 66
Warfighting 9, 11
Westinghouse 31
Wilson, E.O. 86

Xerox 152

Yahoo 54

Zimmerman 151

"Everything is in a state of **change**; nothing endures. We do not seek permanence."

Masatoshi Naito

Matsushita Corp.

About the Author

Idris Mootee is a management consultant specializing in business strategy development, digital strategy development and strategic innovation. He has more than ten years of experience in strategy consulting and has consulted for many corporations large and small around the world. He is a frequent guest speaker at numerous management forums and seminars. For the last five years, his time was spent mostly in London, San Francisco, Boston, New York, Toronto and airport lounges. He is widely respected for his insights, expertise, and ability to infuse organizations with tools for innovation and value creation. His current practice focus is to help companies using the Internet and other emerging technologies to reshape markets, create new industries and increase their potential for innovation that results in value creation as well as helping established companies to transform to e-corporations through comprehensive e-transformation initiatives.